CONTENTS

KV-245-323

HOW TO USE THIS BOOK

This book has been specifically written to prepare students for the Edexcel GCSE Religious Studies paper Unit A Religion and Life, which is based on the study of Christianity and at least one other religion. Because a large number of students choose to study Christianity and Islam, this book has given these two religions equal and detailed coverage. Please note however, religions other than Islam can be studied for the Unit A exam.

The Edexcel exam has a two-hour paper for students who are answering the extended writing options, either Question 9 'Religion and the Media' or Question 10 'Religion: Wealth and Poverty'. These two topics receive extra coverage in the book to help students prepare for those questions adequately. For even more material and activities on all six sections please refer to *Revise for Religious Studies GCSE Edexcel Specification A: Religion and Life* (Heinemann, 2004).

Coursework

Students who choose one of the coursework options sit a one-and-a-half hour exam paper. The two chapters on 'Religion and the Media' and 'Religion: Wealth and Poverty' can be used by students to assist their coursework preparation. There are ideas for personal research with links to websites for up-to-date information, as well as useful addresses to write to for information. The section dedicated to preparing, researching and writing coursework is designed to help students to achieve their best coursework grade.

Exam focus

Every double-page spread has activities designed to help students to develop their analytical and evaluative skills. The activities at the end of each chapter take this a stage further along with specific exam practice. There is one complete section of the book devoted to examples of exam questions for students to practise and helpful advice on how to approach certain types of questions. Using worked examples, students are encouraged to learn how the marking process operates so they can see how marks can be gained or lost. They are also given the chance to 'be the examiner' with examples of varying levels to grade and comment on.

How the book is organised

For ease of use, the textbook follows the Unit A specification, beginning with the philosophical study 'Believing in God'. This is approached from both a Christian and a Muslim perspective so teachers and students can choose which religion to study. This is the only part of the specification that asks for the study of one religion. The religion chosen does not have to be Christianity or Islam.

The title page for each chapter tells a student what the exam paper expects them to know and lists the key terms for the chapter. These key terms with their meanings also reappear throughout the chapter to reinforce learning. The activity that appears on the chapter title page offers a useful introduction to the topic. Each double-page spread is designed to provide the material for a one-hour lesson with activities to develop a student's thinking skills and build towards exam answers.

At the end of each chapter 'Putting it all together' provides three pages of questions to help the student gain an overview of the topic.

Throughout the book the Bible is used as the source of authority for Christians and the Qur'an and Hadith for Muslims. The versions used are the *Good News Bible* and *The Koran with Parallel Arabic Text*, translated by N.J. Dawood.

eligion nd Life

n Christianity and Islam

Unit A

Ina Taylor

www.heinemann.co.uk
✓ Free online support
✓ Useful weblinks
✓ 24 hour online ordering

01865 888058

Heinemann

Inspiring generations

Heinemann Educational Publishers

Halley Court, Jordan Hill, Oxford OX2 8EJ

Part of Harcourt Education

Heinemann is the registered trademark of Harcourt Education Limited

© Ina Taylor, 2005

First published 2005

09 08 07 06
10 9 8 7 6 5 4

British Library Cataloguing in Publication Data is available from the British Library on request.

10-digit ISBN: 0 435 30229 9
13-digit ISBN: 978 0 435302 29 0

Designed and typeset by Artistix

Original illustrations © Harcourt Education Limited, 2005

Illustrated by Andrew Skilleter

Printed in Italy by Printer Trento srl

Cover photo: © Alamy

Picture research by Elaine Willis

Acknowledgements
The author and publisher would like to thank the following for the use of copyright material:

Photographs – pp. 5, 23, 24, 28, 33, 35, 69 (top left), 78, 93, 97, 100, 102, 106 Corbis; pp. 6 (both), 7, 30, 68 (both), 69 (bottom right) Getty Images/ PhotoDisc; p. 8 Harcourt Education/Tudor Photography; pp. 10, 41 (left), 63, 104 Alamy; pp. 13, 50, 51, 59 Ina Taylor; p. 15 SPL; p. 17 Reuters; p. 18 Still Pictures/Christian Aid/Elaine Duigenan; p. 19 Islamic Relief; p. 26 Art Archive; pp. 36, 52 Peter Saunders; pp. 41 (right), 44 Getty; pp. 46, 72, 80 Rex; p. 49 The Children's Society; p. 54 World Religions; p. 60 Equal Opportunities Commission; p. 64 Associated Press; p. 67 PA; p. 70 The Church of England, Diocese of Birmingham; pp. 77, 82, 87 BBC; p. 85 BBC/Karen Wright; p. 88 BBC/Richard Taylor Jones; p. 90 BBC/Rhian AP Gruffyd; pp. 110, 113 (top) Muslim Aid; p. 69 (top right) Getty Images/Digital Vision; p. 94 ITV/Granada; p.108 Muslim Educational Trust; p.114 Still Pictures/Hartmut Scwartzbach.

Realia – p. 16 NSPCC leaflet © NSPCC, photograph posed by models © Matt Harris, p. 61 graph © the Office for National Statistics website; p. 66 table and pie chart © the Office for National Statistics website; p. 80 'It's Madge-ic' © *The Sun*, 20 September 2004; p. 84 TV Guide © PA News Ltd, p. 101 Muslim Aid quote © Muslim Aid; p. 101 Cafod quote © Cafod; p. 105 Cafod quote and logo © Cafod; p. 106 Christian Aid logo © Christian Aid; p. 106 Christian Aid case study © Christian Aid; p. 112 Muslim Aid logo © Muslim Aid; p. 113 Muslim Aid leaflet © Muslim Aid.

Exam questions – Exam questions have been reproduced with the permission of Edexcel Limited. Edexcel Limited accepts no responsibility whatsoever for the accuracy or method of working in the answers given.

Every effort has been made to contact copyright holders of material reproduced in this book. Any omissions will be rectified in subsequent printings if notice is given to the publishers.

1 BELIEVING IN GOD

In this chapter you will learn:

- how religious upbringing in a family or community of Christians or Muslims can lead to, or support, belief in God
- about the nature of religious experience as seen in numinous, conversion, miracles and prayer
- how these religious experiences may lead to, or support, belief in God
- how the appearance of the world (design and causation) may lead to, or support, belief in God
- how the search for meaning and purpose in life may lead to, or support, belief in God
- how the presence of religion in the world may lead to, or support, belief in God
- how non-religious explanations of the world and of miracles may lead to, or support, agnosticism or atheism
- how unanswered prayers and the existence of evil and suffering (including moral evil and natural evil) may lead people to question or reject belief in God

Figure A The night sky.

- why the existence of evil and suffering raises problems for people who believe in God as omnipotent, benevolent and omniscient
- how followers of Christianity and Islam respond to this problem.

NB Unlike the other sections in this book, you only need to study one religion for this section and this does not need to be Christianity. Remember to clearly state what your chosen religion is where appropriate in your answers.

The key terms you must know the meaning of are:

numinous, conversion, miracle, prayer, design argument, causation argument, agnosticism, atheism, moral evil, natural evil, omnipotent, benevolent, omniscient

ACTIVITY

1. Look at Figure A. List some thoughts people might have about the existence, or not, of God if they stared into a night sky. Make a brief note against each point to say why they might think that.

BELIEVING IN GOD

AIM

To understand why some people believe in God, why others do not and why some people are unsure.

KEY TERMS

agnosticism not being sure whether God exists
atheism believing that God does not exist

What happens when I die?

I believe there is a God. There are so many people in the world who believe in the existence of God. Okay, there are lots of different religions, but they accept there is a higher power than us. There is no way they have all got it wrong. In fact there are great similarities in what they all believe even if they live in opposite parts of the globe and have never met. Besides, a lot of people have actually succeeded in communicating with God – **prayer**, that sort of thing – and it has often made a real difference to their lives. Of course God exists. The world didn't happen by accident, did it? The odds on that are far worse than winning the lottery!

Science is marvellous; I'd be the first to agree with that, but science doesn't disprove the existence of God. I think God works through science to help humans. Modern medicine is a perfect example. Can I just say that science will never be able to supply all the answers to everything. For example, there are always cases of people who recover from terrible illnesses that doctors say are untreatable. How do you answer that one? Miracles do happen!

Jessica believes in God.

What is the point of being on earth?

I do not believe in God. I'm an atheist. There's no evidence to convince me that God exists. Science is the way forward. Okay, maybe we don't know everything yet, but new discoveries are being made all the time. Eventually science will answer all our questions.

Miracles? They are just illusions, coincidences. You don't hear people boasting about all the prayers they have made that haven't been answered, do you? Then there are all the terrible disasters that happen where innocent people suffer, now I would say that definitely proves God doesn't exist.

People have made up the idea of a God because they are scared. They don't like the thought that there is nothing out there. It's always comforting to have somebody to turn to when things go wrong, isn't it. It's a bit like being a child really – expecting Mummy to pick you up when you fall over, or cuddle you when you have a bad dream. Grow up! There is nothing there. You've just got to get on with life. What's the point? Well, dare I say it, there isn't one!

Tanvi is an atheist.

I'm not sure whether God exists or not. I'm an agnostic. I'd like to see more proof to be sure there is a God. You say, what about science? Well yes, it's good at explaining how things work. I mean scientists have discovered all sorts of amazing facts about the universe. But let's face it, scientists didn't invent those things, they were already out there. Now surely something must have created them.

I want to know why we are here in the first place. The reason I'm not prepared to come down firmly on one side of the fence or the other is because I know we are only human. How can our brain understand something that is so much more advanced than us? I have trouble getting my head round the idea of what might have existed before the Big Bang!

Ed is an agnostic.

Does good always win over evil?

Why do people suffer when they haven't done anything wrong?

ACTIVITIES

Believer	Agnostic	Atheist

1. Draw a table like the one here, with the headings 'Believer', 'Agnostic', and 'Atheist'. Put the arguments each person on this spread gives for their views in the correct list. As a class, think of other points these three people could have given to add strength to their case.

2. In pairs, choose two of the people and role-play a discussion between them. Remember each is keen to convince the other one that they are right!

3. With a partner, decide what answers a **believer** and an atheist would give to the questions on this spread.

4. Answer these questions.

a) What is meant by the word 'atheist'?

b) Outline the reasons a person might give for being agnostic.

☺ For discussion

'God must exist because, so many people believe.' Would you agree with this statement? Is it possible that such a large number of people have got it wrong?

1 A Christian upbringing

AIM

To understand why a Christian upbringing might lead to or support belief in God.

KEY TERMS

benevolent the belief that God is good/kind
omnipotent the belief that God is all-powerful
omniscient the belief that God knows everything that has happened and everything that is going to happen
prayer an attempt to contact God, usually through words

STARTER

Discuss with a partner why you think the teenagers in Figure B have chosen to go to church. What two questions would you like to ask them?

In the family

A person born into a Christian family is likely to be taken to church from the age of a few months. Some Christians baptize their children into the religion at a young age, and the parents and godparents promise to bring the child up as a Christian. This means the child will be taught to pray and might take part in daily worship at home with their family.

Families usually celebrate the main Christian festivals of Easter and Christmas in the home as well as in the church, and children are taught the meaning and importance of these festivals. They might learn some of the Gospel stories associated with the festival and sing special carols at this time.

Some Christian parents arrange for their children to attend a church school where there is a greater emphasis on learning about Christianity and encouragement to lead a Christian life.

Figure B Why do you think worship plays an important role in a Christian family?

In the community

As a Christian, a person is likely to be a member of the community centred on a place of worship such as the church. They will probably worship there with their family every Sunday and younger children might attend Sunday school to learn more about their religion. Mixing with other Christians gives them the opportunity to discuss their faith and learn from the experiences and teachings of others. Most people find it strengthens their faith to worship in a group rather than on their own. As a member of a Christian community, a person might be encouraged to put Jesus' teachings into practice by undertaking charity work.

Why might this support a person's belief in God?

Being born into a Christian family might support someone's belief in God because they are surrounded by others who are convinced of the existence of God. If the religion had been handed down the generations it might seem perfectly natural to members of that family to believe in God. Learning about God at home, at school and in church could lead some people to decide God must exist.

FOR RESEARCH

Find out what confirmation is. Why do you think someone brought up as a Christian might want to be confirmed? How might this strengthen their belief in God?

The basic Christian beliefs about God

- Christians believe there is only one God who wishes good for everyone. God is **benevolent**.
- God is more powerful than anything else. God is **omnipotent**.
- Christians believe God has great knowledge and knows everything that is going on at the moment, in the past and what will happen in the future. God is **omniscient**.
- Christians believe that humans still have the freedom to behave as they choose. God may know what people are going to do but God does not control their actions. Humans are not puppets.

For discussion

'Everyone is entitled to free will when it comes to religion.' Why? Would you let a two-year-old exercise her free will about attending the family service at church? Why?

ACTIVITIES

1. Draw a table with two columns: 'Features of a Christian upbringing' and 'Effects of a Christian upbringing'. Use the information on these pages, along with any more points you can think of, to fill in the column. Against each of your points write the likely outcome in the right-hand column. Which do you think is likely to be the most influential in leading someone to believe in God? Could any of the points have the opposite effect? If so, why?

2. Cut out six pieces of paper. Write the words 'omniscient', 'omnipotent' and 'benevolent' on three of the pieces. On the other three pieces copy down the meaning of each word. Shuffle the papers up, then match the correct word to its meaning. Do this several times to ensure that you understand what each word means.

3. As a class, discuss whether you think children should be allowed to make up their own minds about whether or not to believe in God.

4. What answers do you think the teenagers in Figure B would give to your questions from the starter?

AIM

To understand why an Islamic upbringing might lead to or support belief in God.

KEY TERMS

omnipotent the belief that God is all-powerful
omniscient the belief that God knows everything that has happened and everything that is going to happen
prayer an attempt to contact God, usually through words

STARTER

Discuss with a partner why you think the teenagers in Figure C are taking part in family worship. What two questions would you like to ask them?

In the family

Muslims believe that everyone born into an Islamic family is a Muslim. Islam is a way of life as much as a religion and it is every parent's duty to teach their children how to become good Muslims. No ceremony is necessary to make a baby a Muslim, however it is usual for there to be a ceremony soon after the birth of a baby. The father, or a respected male member of the community, whispers the adhan, the call to prayer, into the baby's ear. This is so the first word a Muslim hears when they enter the world is 'God'.

In the home children are taught the five pillars of Islam. These are the basic rules of life for a Muslim. They are encouraged from an early age to join the family for prayers five times a day. Children are usually taught how to lead a good Muslim life, which involves behaving correctly and dressing modestly, as well as eating the permitted food.

Figure C An Islamic family at prayer. Can you suggest why this might be an important part of daily life for Muslims? How might this experience of prayer influence a child to believe in God?

The main Islamic festivals of Id-ul-Adha and Id-ul-Fitr are celebrated in the home. Members of the extended family meet together at festival times and children learn the origins and religious importance of the occasion from older relatives.

PATH TO THE TOP

Find out more about the Aqiqah Ceremony to welcome a baby into the family. Could this support belief in God? For the baby? For the family?

In the community

The Muslim community, the **ummah**, does its best to encourage all members to follow the path of Islam. The local ummah is likely to centre on the mosque where the men and boys join other male Muslims in communal prayer every Friday. Mixing with other Muslims gives young boys the chance to discuss their faith and learn from others. Girls are most likely to worship at home with their mother and the younger members of the family.

After they have finished their day at school, Muslim children usually attend the **madrasah**, mosque school, to learn about Islam. In some instances Muslim children are able to attend a Muslim day school but there are not many of these in Britain.

Why might this support a Muslim's belief in God?

Being born into a Muslim family is likely to support a Muslim's belief in God because they are surrounded by others who are convinced of God's existence. Muslim children are brought up to lead an Islamic way of life, so it might seem perfectly natural to them to believe in God. Having the chance to learn about God at home, at school and in the mosque would reinforce their belief in God's existence.

Basic Islamic beliefs about God

- Muslims believe there is only one God, who created the world and everything in it. God is more powerful than anything in existence: omnipotent.
- God knows what is going on at the moment, in the past and what will happen in the future: omniscient.
- God might know what people are going to do, but Muslims believe God does not control their actions.
- God gave Prophet Muhammad the Qur'an, a book, that contains the words of God and gives Muslims all the information necessary to lead a perfect life.

ACTIVITIES

1. Draw a table with two columns: 'Features of a Muslim upbringing' and 'Effects of a Muslim upbringing'. Use the information on these pages, along with any more points you can think of, to fill in the column 'Features of a Muslim upbringing'. Against each of your points write the likely outcome in the right-hand column. Which do you think is likely to be the most influential in supporting a Muslim's belief in God? Could any of the points have the opposite effect? If so, why?

2. As a class discuss whether you think children should be allowed to make up their own minds about whether or not to believe in God.

3. Based on what you have learned about a Muslim upbringing, what answers do you think the teenagers in Figure C would give to your questions at the start of this lesson?

1 It's personal!

AIM

To understand why some religious experiences might lead to or support a person's faith in God.

KEY TERMS

conversion when your life is changed by giving yourself to God

miracle something which seems to break a law of science and makes you think only God could have done it

numinous the feeling of the presence of something greater than you, e.g. in a church or looking up at the stars

prayer an attempt to contact God, usually through words

The 'wow' factor!

Some people arrive at a belief in God without the assistance of their family or friends. Something happens to them that takes them by surprise and convinces them that there is a God. For some it might be the 'wow!' factor; they see something which completely takes their breath away and gives them a feeling of awe and wonder. This convinces them that they are in the presence of a greater power. The feeling is called the **numinous**. Some people experience it when they enter a religious building; for others it comes from a marvel of nature – a glorious sunset, the intricacy of a snowflake seen through a microscope or being present when a new life enters the world.

For some people this experience is so powerful it convinces them that God exists. There are others who are so profoundly moved by the experience that their life is never the same again. They undergo a religious **conversion**, which means they commit themselves to one particular religion and strive to serve God by following the ways of that religion closely.

Prayer

Prayer is the most important and personal way for a religious person to communicate with God. Prayers may vary from giving thanks, to praising God or asking God for help. On occasions people believe their prayers are answered; maybe the sick person they asked God to heal, does get better, or the problem they asked for God's guidance on is solved. If a prayer is answered, that person's belief in God is strengthened.

When a prayer is not answered as a believer hoped, then their faith can be challenged. It might lead some to wonder whether God exists or not, and become an agnostic. An unanswered prayer might convince others that God does not exist and lead them to become an atheist. Some believers would argue that God does listen to everyone's prayers and responds in the way He sees fit. Humans cannot possibly understand the mind of God.

For discussion

How do you think a believer would feel if they were not healed even though they had prayed to God?

ACTIVITY

1. Read an account of Yusuf Islam (the former pop singer, Cat Stevens) and his conversion to Islam by visiting the Heinemann website at www.heinemann.co.uk/hotlinks. Type in the express code 2299P and clicking on this section to access the relevant website. Devise four questions you would like to ask him so you can understand his religious experience better.

PATH TO THE TOP

A useful term you might use is **mystical experience**, which means hearing God's voice or seeing a vision of a religious figure. Look up Acts 9: 1–31. What mystical experience convinced Saul to believe in God and become the apostle St. Paul?

Figure D Some people's belief in God is triggered by the natural world. The feeling of awe and wonder they experience, which is called the numinous, convinces them there is a greater power at work in the world. They believe that power is God.

Miracles

Miracles often cause controversy because they are paranormal happenings which break the natural laws of science. There are well-documented cases of people praying to God for help and then, for example, recovering from an illness which medical science had said was incurable. There can be other miraculous happenings when, against all the odds, someone survives a natural disaster. For example, there have been instances of people, even babies, being rescued from the debris of a collapsed building several days after it had been destroyed by an earthquake.

Christians believe God can perform miracles. They point to evidence of miracles in both the Old Testament and the New Testament and to the fact that Jesus himself performed many miracles of healing and miracles over nature. For Christians, Jesus' **resurrection** from the dead was the greatest miracle of all.

Many Muslims also believe in miracles but in Islam the greatest miracle is the revelation of the Qur'an. The fact that the words of God have been given to humans for their guidance is the miracle.

The effect of miracles

People who witness miracles are usually convinced they are seeing the work of God and their faith is strengthened.

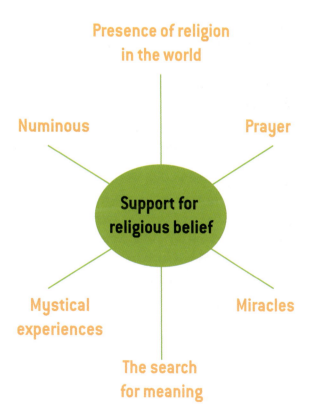

Presence of religion in the world

Numinous

Prayer

Support for religious belief

Mystical experiences

Miracles

The search for meaning

ACTIVITY

2. Revise how the Qur'an was given to humanity. Why do Muslims believe the Qur'an is a miracle?

AIM

To understand how the appearance of the world may lead some people to believe in God and others to reach a non-religious conclusion.

KEY TERMS

causation argument the idea that everything has been caused (started off) by something else
design argument when things are connected and seem to have a purpose, e.g. the eye is designed for seeing

STARTER

Think of a designer garment. Make a list of the features that show that this item was produced by a high-quality designer.

The design argument

William Paley put forward the **design argument** several hundred years ago. He said if somebody happened to find a watch and had never seen one before in their life, they would be astounded.

The fact that something so tiny had such an intricate mechanism would lead them to believe that it had been made by a very clever person. Nothing like that could possibly happen by accident. Paley said the same argument could be applied to the universe, which is far more complicated than any watch mechanism. It could never have happened by chance, it must have been designed by an extremely clever being. The only possible designer is God. That proves God exists, he reasoned.

ACTIVITY

1. What do you think Paley would say if someone asked him about the reason for earthquakes?

The causation argument

If something unexpected happens we always try to see what has caused it. If a jug falls off the table, or a car veers across the road, most people look for the cause of that action. 'Things do not happen by themselves,' they say.

The **causation argument** says that the mere existence of the universe is proof God exists. If the universe had a beginning then something must have caused it. The universe did not happen by accident and only something as powerful as God could have brought it into existence. That proves God exists.

ACTIVITY

2. Working with a partner, try to come up with three things that might happen without anyone or anything causing them. Share your ideas with the class.

The argument for the Big Bang

This widely accepted scientific theory for the beginning of the universe states that around fifteen billion years ago there was a cosmic explosion – a 'big bang'. Gases and matter were thrown apart at virtually the speed of light. Our universe was formed as gases cooled. Support for this theory is found in the way the galaxies are continuing to move away from each other and that echoes of the Big Bang can be picked up today by powerful radio telescopes.

ACTIVITY

3. What would the supporters of the causation argument say about the Big Bang theory?

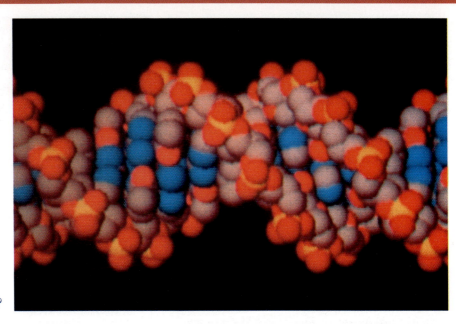

Figure E Scientists have worked out that this is the model of DNA, the structure of life. Many people think our understanding of DNA is the most important discovery of the past hundred years. We would never have known of its existence without scientists, but they did not invent DNA. It has always been there since the beginning of time. Did DNA happen by chance?

The argument for natural selection

Darwin's theory of evolution by natural selection states that over millions of years plant and animal life has adapted to its environment. Plants and animals were not necessarily created in the form we see them today. They have evolved and continue to do so. Each adaptation is passed on to their offspring and those organisms that fail to change simply die out. Only the species which are the fittest and best suited to the changing conditions on the planet will survive.

💬 For discussion

'Some people say you cannot believe in evolution and God. Well I think that God has to use evolution to create intelligent life. Humans have got to think for themselves or they would just be programmed like mini computers.' As a class discuss the point this scientist is making.

FOR RESEARCH

- List four ways in which we use DNA today.
- Work out why our knowledge of DNA might lead some people to believe in the existence of God.
- Work out why our knowledge of DNA might lead other people to conclude that God does not exist.
- Does a person's DNA tell you everything you need to know about them?

ACTIVITY

4. a) Write down your thoughts on why each of the arguments on this spread might lead some people to believe in God.
b) Look at each argument again and decide why it might lead an atheist to say God does not exist.
c) How would an agnostic react to each of the arguments?

1 Evil is a problem

AIM

To understand why the existence of evil and suffering can cause problems for those who believe in God.

KEY TERMS

moral evil actions done by humans which cause suffering

natural evil things which cause suffering but have nothing to do with humans, e.g. earthquakes

STARTER

With a partner look at Figures F and G. What differences are there between these forms of suffering? Who might be to blame in each case? Is it possible either of them could have been avoided?

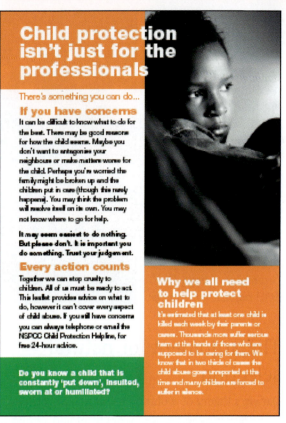

Child protection isn't just for the professionals

There's something you can do...

If you have concerns

It can be difficult to know what to do for the best. There may be good reasons for how the child seems. Maybe you don't want to antagonise your neighbours or make matters worse for the child. Perhaps you're worried the family might be broken up and the children put in care (though this rarely happens). You may think the problem will resolve itself on its own. You may not know where to go for help.

It may seem easiest to do nothing. But please don't. It is important you do something. Trust your judgement.

Every action counts

Together we can stop cruelty to children. All of us must be ready to act. This leaflet provides advice on what to do, however it can't cover every aspect of child abuse. If you still have concerns you can always telephone or email the NSPCC Child Protection Helpline, for free 24-hour advice.

Do you know a child that is constantly 'put down', insulted, sworn at or humiliated?

Why we all need to help protect children

It's estimated that at least one child is killed each week by their parents or carer. Thousands more suffer serious harm at the hands of those who are supposed to be caring for them. We know that in two thirds of cases the child abuse goes unreported at the time and many children are forced to suffer in silence.

(photograph posed by models © Matt Harris)

***Figure F** Most people think hurting children is one of the worst forms of moral evil. Why is hurting a child worse than hurting an adult?*

The big problem

One of the difficulties people have when they consider whether God exists or not is understanding why suffering happens.

Moral evil

Moral evil is suffering caused by people. The suffering is caused by someone who knows what they were doing and intends to cause harm. A religious believer might find it difficult to understand why God created people who were capable of doing such evil.

Moral evil can also happen accidentally. The driver who falls asleep at the wheel and crashes into children walking along the pavement causes great suffering.

ACTIVITY

1. List four more situations you would say involve moral evil.

What is the problem?

When cases of child cruelty come to light people immediately start asking questions and try to apportion blame. The usual questions are 'Who did this?' and 'Why did it happen?' Some people might ask a deeper question about why God allows such things to happen. If you look back to pages 8–9 and 11, you will notice that God is described as benevolent, omniscient and omnipotent.

- Believers find it hard to understand how a God who is said to be benevolent (in other words good and kind) can allow suffering to happen to people.
- Some suggest that perhaps the answer is that God is not omnipotent after all. Perhaps God is not powerful enough to prevent evil happening.

Figure G This devastation was caused by the Tsunami on 26 December 2004. An earthquake in the Indian Ocean caused tidal waves of such size and force that people living near the coast could not escape. At least 225 thousand people are estimated to have died that day across 11 nations, making it the worse natural disaster in history.

- Other people question whether God really is omniscient. They say if God does know everything about the past, present and future, then God would have known this was going to happen and could have stopped it.
- People who are faithful believers and communicate with God through prayer might wonder why their prayers have gone unanswered when this sort of thing happens.
- If God created everything in the universe, did God create evil?
- An atheist might argue that these events happen because God does not exist at all.

Natural evil

Natural evil is, as the name suggests, caused by nature. It might take the form of an earthquake, volcanic eruption, drought or tidal wave. It can often result in widespread suffering when people are injured and made homeless by a disaster. Believers find it hard to understand why such disasters happen to innocent people.

For discussion

Look at the problems highlighted by bullet points on these pages and decide how many also apply to natural evil.

ACTIVITIES

2. a) Divide your page into two columns. In one column note down the argument in favour of a designer God. In the other column note down the case against a designer God based on natural evil.

b) Underneath write one sentence stating whether you think the existence of evil and suffering leads you to believe or disbelieve in God.

c) Write a final sentence explaining why you have come to that conclusion.

3. Either watch the national and local news on television one evening and note down all the stories which involve suffering, or go through a copy of a newspaper and cut out ten stories that involve suffering.

4. Sort your stories into instances of moral evil and natural evil. Not every situation is clearly one or the other. Some cases of suffering may be a mixture of the two. War, which might be a moral evil, could lead to a crop failure in the region and a famine. Go through each and decide who, or what, caused the incident and whether it could have been avoided.

AIM

To understand how Christians and Muslims respond to the problems of evil and suffering.

KEY TERMS

prayer   an attempt to contact God, usually through words

STARTER

As a class, make a list of the problems that evil and suffering cause religious believers.

What do Christians believe are the reasons for evil and suffering?

Christians differ in their views about the causes of evil and suffering.

- Some believe that God created a perfect world for humanity, but Adam and Eve used their free will to disobey God. Their punishment resulted in humans being separated from God. This has led to suffering and evil. God sent Jesus to die for the sins of humanity, rise again, and bring people back to God.
- Others believe God created people with free will and because people are not programmed like computers, they can choose whether to do good or evil. When they choose evil, suffering occurs.
- To some Christians, life is a test. The way people react to suffering and evil determines whether they go to heaven or hell in the afterlife (see page 27).
- Others say that God does have reasons for permitting suffering and evil but humans will never be able to understand the mind of God.

Figure H A Christian charity has provided this Afghan village with piped water. Villagers used to have half a day's walk to the nearest supply. Which part of the quotation from Matthew 25 are these Christians putting into practice?

In responding to the problems of evil, Christians are guided by the teachings and actions of Jesus, who taught his followers:

- to use prayer to ask for God's help; Jesus prayed to God his father for strength to face the evil that would kill him.
- to be of service to those who are suffering; Jesus helped the sick and dying.

According to the Bible, Jesus said:

I was hungry and you fed me, thirsty and you gave me a drink; I was a stranger and you received me in your homes, naked and you clothed me; I was sick and you took care of me, in prison and you visited me ... I tell you, whenever you did this for one of the least important of these members of my family, you did it for me!' (Matthew 25: 35–40)

FOR RESEARCH

Find out more about the work of Christian Aid. Whereabouts in the world are they currently working? Go to www.heinemann.co.uk/hotlinks, type in the express code 2299P and click on this section to access the Christian Aid website.

What do Muslims believe are the reasons for evil and suffering?

- Muslims believe that life is a test. On the Day of Judgement, God weighs up everyone's good and bad deeds and decides whether that person goes to paradise or to hell.

- God has a plan for everyone and suffering may be part of it. There is always a reason for suffering but humans cannot know the mind of God.

- Evil was created by Shaytan, a fallen angel. God permits Shaytan and evil to exist in order to test people.

- God gives everyone free will. The Qur'an teaches that God wants people to submit to the will of God, but everyone has a choice. Some will reject God and choose evil.

The Qur'an teaches that Muslims should accept suffering as a test set by God. They should not question it or fight against it. No one is given more suffering than they can cope with and their suffering will bring them closer to God. Muslims submit to God through prayer and by following the teachings of the Qur'an and the practice of Muhammad. The way they react to suffering will be judged. **Zakah**, the third pillar of Islam, teaches Muslims to give money to the poor and needy to relieve suffering.

The Hadith says:

He is not a believer who eats his fill while his neighbour remains hungry by his side.

An ignorant person who is generous is nearer to Allah than a person full of prayer who is miserly.

If anyone supplies a need to any one of my people, desiring to please him by it, he has pleased me; and he who has pleased me has pleased Allah; and he who has pleased Allah will be brought to Paradise.

Figure 1 *This Muslim charity relieves suffering in Iran following an earthquake.*

FOR RESEARCH

There are many Muslim charities which help relieve suffering such as Islamic Relief, Muslim Aid and Red Crescent. More details of their work appear on their websites which can be accessed via www.heinemann.co.uk/hotlinks. Type in the express code 2299P and click on this section to visit the three websites.

ACTIVITIES

1. 'Suffering has a purpose,' said the 400 metre Olympic hopeful during training. With a partner discuss what the sprinter meant. Contrast his view with the attitude of either a Christian or a Muslim towards suffering. Do you agree with what the sprinter said?

2. Cut out a picture of natural evil and another of moral evil from a newspaper or magazine and stick them in the centre of a plain A4 sheet to make a poster. Label the natural evil and the moral evil. Write what a Muslim or a Christian might say about the suffering in your picture. Include a quotation from a sacred text if you can.

ACTIVITIES

1. Visit www.heinemann.co.uk/hotlinks, type in the express code 2299P and click on this section for information about Islamia, one of the Islamic schools in Britain. How could attendance there reinforce a Muslim's belief in God?

2. Find out more about the religious experiences some Christians claim to have had from a pilgrimage to Lourdes by visiting www.heinemann.co.uk/hotlinks, typing in the express code 2299P and clicking on this section. How might these experiences support a belief in God?

3. Make an A3 poster that demonstrates the causation argument. Include in your poster a panel explaining clearly why this argument might lead some people to believe in God.

4. You have been asked to prepare the opening questions for a celebrity interviewer in a television chat show. One of his guests is a well-known Muslim astronomer and the other a space technician from NASA who is an atheist. The interviewer needs to get his guests arguing. Give him three questions to start things off.

5. Sort these arguments into two columns. Head one column 'Arguments to support a belief in God'. Head the other column 'Arguments against the existence of God'.

- Miracles are just illusions. Science will soon be able to prove that.
- Miracles do occur and God is the only satisfactory explanation for this.
- If God is supposed to be good and powerful why does he not heal everybody who is sick, rather than just perform a few miracle cures?
- Personal religious experiences are all in the mind; there is no God.
- Personal religious experiences are all in the mind, which is where God communicates with believers.
- Miracles are one way in which God answers the prayers of believers.
- Miracles are just another name for luck or coincidence.

Tackling an exam question

Here is a **(b)** question from the exam paper.

> Outline the view that evil and suffering are a problem for religious believers. **(6)**

HINT
Pages 16–17 will refresh your memory on this subject. The **(b)** question is asking you to give facts and then show how they apply to a religion. In this case, no specific religion has been mentioned.

Planning your answer to this question

1. Go through and underline the important words in this question. This will focus your mind and stop you wandering off the point: <u>Outline</u>, <u>evil and suffering</u>, <u>problem for religious believers</u>.

2. Analyse the question. <u>Evil and suffering</u> and <u>problem</u> are key terms in this question. The question is asking you to outline what problems they cause. Do not go into great detail; just get the main points down. As part of your planning for this answer go back to pages 16–17 and list the points a religious believer is going to be concerned about.

3. <u>Religious believers</u> are also important to this question, so you need to be clear why they, more than non-believers, are going to have problems with evil and suffering. In what ways does the existence of evil challenge the beliefs of religious people?

4. Note down any key terms that appeared in this part of the specification. If you can use some specialist terms in your answer it might raise your level because it shows you have a good understanding of the issue.

Student's answer

Lots of people say God doesn't exist because of all the terrible things that happen in the world. But I think they are wrong. It is people that get the guns and shoot innocent people outside clubs. You can't blame God for that. Then there are floods which kill people. Who started them? I do not believe in God so I wouldn't say it was him. ✓ (Level 1)

Examiner's comments

The student clearly did not sort out the important parts of this question. The answer started off well with a good example of relevant information in his first sentence, but then he wandered off the point. The answer lacks structure and the student has even given things he was not asked for, such as his opinion of the problem! This answer does not get beyond Level 1. To improve his answer, the student needs to briefly say how a Muslim or Christian would react to evil and suffering. Then he must link this to the believer's view of God and explain why this might cause a problem.

Level 1 (2 marks)
For an isolated example of relevant knowledge.

Level 2 (4 marks)
For basic relevant knowledge presented within a limited structure.

Level 3 (6 marks)
For an organised outline/description, using relevant knowledge with limited use of specialist vocabulary.

Student's improved answer

Lots of people say God doesn't exist because of all the terrible things that happen in the world. Christians believe that God is benevolent so they might find it difficult to understand why a God who loves people would allow suffering to happen. ✓ (L1)

Many religious believers who think God is omniscient and omnipotent would not be able to understand why God doesn't stop evil when he knows it is going to happen. ✓ (L2)

Believers who have prayed to God to help them through their suffering would also find it hard to understand why their prayers weren't answered. ✓ (L3)

1 a) A clear definition is required (see p. 6).

b) Take care to answer from only one religion. Say which one it is. Pages 8–11 will help you.

c) Remember to say what the religious experiences might be **and** how that affects a person's belief in God (see pp. 12–13). There are two parts to this answer! Help with this sort of question appears on page 123.

d) This is your chance to give a personal opinion. Say what you think and why. Then say what other people think and why they say it. Pages 14–15 will help with scientific ideas and page 123 with this sort of argumentative answer.

Questions 1(b) and 2(b) are taken from Edexcel Unit A paper 2004. Questions 1(c) and 2(d) are based on questions from the Edexcel Unit A Specimen Paper.

SECTION ONE: BELIEVING IN GOD
You must answer ONE question from this section.

EITHER QUESTION 1

1 a) What does *atheism* mean? **(2)**

b) Choose **ONE** religion and describe the main features of a religious upbringing in that religion. **(6)**

c) Explain why religious experiences might lead to or support a belief in God. **(8)**

d) "Modern science makes it impossible to believe in God."
Do you agree? Give reasons for your opinion, showing you have considered another point of view. **(4)**

(Total 20 marks)

OR QUESTION 2

2 a) What does *conversion* mean? **(2)**

b) Outline an argument for God's existence based on the appearance of design in the world. **(6)**

c) Explain why the existence of evil and suffering in the world leads some people to become atheists. **(8)**

d) "Children should be allowed to make up their own minds about whether to believe in God or not."
Do you agree? Give reasons for your answer showing you have considered another point of view. **(4)**

(Total 20 marks)

Leave blank

Q1

---

2 a) Keep your definition brief (see p. 12).

b) Be concise (no waffle) but get all the points down (see pp. 14–15).

c) There are two parts to this answer. First state the problem, then the effect that has on some people's beliefs (see pp. 16–17). Page 122 gives help with **(c)** questions.

d) Your views are required so you could begin 'I think ... because ...' Then give the other side's views 'Other people think ... because ...' You must come to a conclusion (which could be that you are not sure) showing you have considered another viewpoint. See page 123 for help with **(d)** questions.

2 MATTERS OF LIFE AND DEATH

In this chapter you will learn:

- about Christian teachings on life after death, including resurrection and the immortality of the soul
- about Muslim teachings on life after death
- why Christians and Muslims believe in life after death
- why people of no specific religion believe in life after death, including near-death experiences and the paranormal
- why some people do not believe in life after death
- about the nature of abortion including current British legislation and non-religious arguments concerning abortion
- about Christian and Muslim teachings concerning abortion, euthanasia and the sanctity of life
- about the nature of euthanasia (assisted suicide, voluntary and non-voluntary euthanasia), current British legislation and non-religious arguments concerning euthanasia.

Figure A *Paramedics face life and death situations on a daily basis. Do you think they would be helped by a belief in God? Why?*

The key terms you must know are:

resurrection, immortality of the soul, paranormal, abortion, sanctity of life, euthanasia, assisted suicide, voluntary euthanasia, non-voluntary euthanasia

ACTIVITY

1. Look at Figure A above. With a partner, discuss whether you think it is always right to try to resuscitate a very sick patient. Explain your answer. Are there any situations where you think preserving life at all costs is questionable? Why?

2 What's next?

AIM

To understand and evaluate the arguments for and against a belief in life after death.

KEY TERMS

paranormal unexplained things which are thought to have spiritual causes, e.g. ghosts and mediums

STARTER

Look back to pages 6 and 7 and the definitions of atheism, agnosticism and believer in the glossary. Decide what each person would say about the idea of life after death.

A recent survey in Britain showed that 70 per cent of the population thought there was some sort of life after death. Interestingly, the majority of those questioned did not belong to any religion.

The case for life after death

- People have experienced **paranormal** activities, i.e. things which are thought to have a supernatural cause.

- Mind over matter – the mind can make the body do impossible things, such as walk barefoot over red hot coals without getting burnt. On occasions the mind can persuade the body to heal itself of an 'incurable' illness. Scientists agree that the brain is extremely powerful and we do not fully understand how it works.

- The brain is separate from the body. For instance, we can imagine all sorts of conflicting emotions in the mind that we have never experienced. Also, the body can live on after the mind is dead, e.g. a person on a life-support machine can be brain-dead.

- People from all parts of the world and from all sorts of religions, as well as those with no religion at all, have believed in life after death since earliest times. Are they all wrong?

Figure B *The Victorians used trick photography to try and convince people that there was life after death. Do you think science could ever be used to prove, or disprove something supernatural? Why? Do you think that if you believe in life after death, you have to believe in ghosts?*

Paranormal experiences

- Near-death experiences – these have been reported in cases where a patient was pronounced clinically dead for a brief time, then revived. Such people tell of remarkably similar experiences such as travelling through a tunnel towards a bright light and peace. Usually they never reach the light because they are revived and have to return to life. Most who have had this experience said they did not want to come back to earth. Often their experience profoundly changed their attitude to life. They were convinced they had seen evidence of the existence of God and of life after death so they no longer feared death.

- There is a widespread belief in the existence of ghosts, who are thought to be the spirits of dead people that are sometimes visible to the living. Ghosts seem to be there for a purpose. Some haunt the living, some are said to give warnings and others just wander around without making contact with the living.

What do you think about this?

One suggestion is that that our brain is like a computer which operates the human body. It is powered by an energy force you could call the mind. This energy is separate from the brain in the same way that electricity is separate from the computer it operates. Switch a computer off and it goes dead, but the electricity is still there even if it is not being used. Do you think this image could be applied to the human brain? Could there be an energy force which continues to exist after the body has died?

The case against life after death

- Scientific evidence shows that when the body dies, everything decays.
- No one has returned from the dead to tell us.
- The end of life means exactly that. It is illogical to speak about life after death.
- Life-support machines prove the brain dies before the body.

The case against the paranormal

Those who disagree with the idea of the paranormal believe that it is all imagination. People who desperately wish to make contact with someone they loved who has died probably knew them well enough to be able to visualise their presence and know what they might say.

Stories of near-death experiences are similar because they are hallucinations conjured up by a dying brain as it closes down. They are simply a chemical reaction to oxygen starvation. It is similar to a computer going through various closing-down functions as it is switched off. It is also well known that some drugs given to patients undergoing surgery can produce weird dreams.

The US Navy conducted experiments to find out how much gravitational force their pilots could withstand before they passed out. Several reported that just before they lost consciousness they experienced tunnel vision, saw bright lights and felt a sense of exhilaration. One major difference, however, was that none of the pilots were changed by their experience nor felt it was evidence of life after death.

ACTIVITIES

1. Divide your page into two columns. List arguments for and against a belief in life after death. Prepare a presentation to show the contrasting views people hold. Include the atheist's view. You could use PowerPoint to display your presentation.

2. What would you ask a person claiming to have had a near-death experience, if they were appearing on a television chat show? Why do you think viewers would be interested in their experience?

2 The Christian view of life after death

AIM

To understand and evaluate different Christian attitudes towards teachings about life after death.

KEY TERMS

immortality of the soul the idea that the soul lives on after the death of the body

resurrection the belief that, after death, the body stays in the grave until the end of the world when it is raised

STARTER

Look at Figure C and look up Luke 24: 37–9. How did Jesus explain to his followers that he was a bodily resurrection and not a ghostly apparition? Do you think the artist intended the picture to show exactly what happened? What might people mean when they say the picture (and the story in Luke) is symbolic?

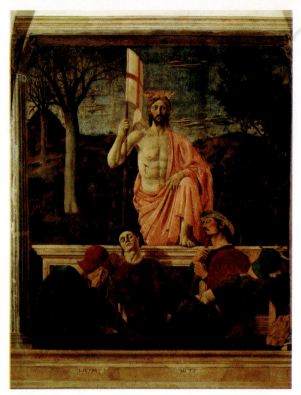

***Figure C** The resurrection of Jesus is the single most important reason why Christians believe in the life after death.*

Life after death

All Christians believe there is life after death and that they will be judged on their actions in this life because that was what Jesus taught. However, Christians differ in their understanding of the form life after death will take. Look at the page opposite for some of the most widely held beliefs.

ACTIVITIES

1. In a group of four, divide 1 Corinthians 15 into four sections. Each person should work through a section, noting down what St Paul said about life after death. Come together as a group to consider how Christians might interpret these teachings.

2. Create a mind map to help you revise the different interpretations of life after death within Christianity.

PATH TO THE TOP

A useful concept you could use to help you achieve higher grades is the **communion of saints**.

'Communion' in this context means community and the word 'saints' is used to mean all Christians, alive or dead, on earth and in heaven. Some Christians believe that it is possible for those on earth to pray to those in heaven to ask for guidance or to ask them to speak to God.

HINT

Remember there is a wide variation in Christian beliefs about the subject of life after death. For instance, some Christians would not accept material about the paranormal as evidence of anything. Not all Christians believe in the existence of hell either because they say a loving God would never allow such evil to exist. To be on the safe side always say, 'Some Christians believe…'

Life after death

Resurrection

Some evangelical Protestants believe that, after death, the body stays in the grave and nothing happens until the Last Day at the end of the world. Then every body will be raised from the dead and brought before God for judgement. The good will go to heaven for eternity and those who have sinned, and never repented, will be sent to hell for eternity.

Reasons for this belief:

- the body of Jesus was raised from the dead
- the **Creed** says, 'I believe in the resurrection of the body and the life everlasting'
- the Bible says, 'When the body is buried, it is mortal; when raised, it will be immortal … When buried, it is a physical body; when raised, it will be a spiritual body'. [1 Corinthians 15: 42 and 44]

Purgatory

Roman Catholics believe that after death the souls of those who have led blameless lives will go straight to heaven. Those who have sinned will enter a state of waiting and preparation for heaven; there the soul will be cleansed. They call it **purgatory**. Those who have committed great evil and not repented will go to hell for eternity.

On the Last Day, Jesus will return to earth and raise the dead from their graves and reunite them with their souls. Then God will judge everyone.

Reasons for this belief:

- Jesus rose from the dead
- the Creed states that Jesus rose again on the third day and 'is seated at the right hand of the Father and will come again to judge the living and the dead'
- the Bible says, 'For God loved the world so much that he gave his only Son, so that everyone who believes in him may not die but have eternal life'. [John 3: 16]

Immortality of the soul

Other Protestants believe that after death the body will stay in the grave but the soul will be taken straight to God to be judged. People who have been good will stay with God. There is a difference of opinion about the fate of those who have sinned. Some believe they will be sent to a place called hell, others think there is no such place. Simply to be separated from God is hell.

Reasons for this belief:

- Jesus told the thief crucified alongside him, 'I promise you that today you will be in Paradise with me' [Luke 23: 43]
- Jesus also told his followers, 'There are many rooms in my Father's house, and I am going to prepare a place for you … I will come back and take you to myself, so that you will be where I am' [John 14: 2–3]
- the Creed states, 'I believe in the communion of saints … and the life everlasting'. By 'communion' Christians mean a bond between all Christians alive and dead
- some Christians believe paranormal experiences such as ghosts are evidence of the **immortality of the soul**
- others say the teaching of the Bible is the only evidence needed of the immortality of the soul.

KEY TERMS

immortality of the soul the idea that the soul lives on after the death of the body

resurrection the belief that, after death, the body stays in the grave until the end of the world when it is raised

What do Muslims believe?

There is no doubt in the mind of any Muslim that life after death exists. Belief in life after death, **akhirah**, is one of the three most important concepts in Islam (the others being belief in one God and belief in Muhammad as the final messenger of God). Anyone who doubts the existence of life after death is not a Muslim, the Qur'an says.

Muslims believe that, once they die, their body goes into the ground and remains there until the Last Day. During the waiting period that follows, the angel of death takes the soul to **barzakh** (a waiting area) until such time as God ends the world. On the Last Day God will resurrect every body from their grave. Body and soul will be reunited to go before God for judgement. Everyone will be judged on the way they behaved on earth.

Figure D The Qur'an (98: 8) says that the reward for those who are faithful to God will be, 'the gardens of Eden, gardens watered by running streams, where they shall dwell for ever'. This photograph is of the beautiful Generalife gardens at the Alhambra in Granada, Spain, created by Muslims many years ago as a paradise on earth. It is hardly surprising that a religion which began in the desert regions of Saudi Arabia should imagine heaven to be like a fertile water garden. What else might these gardens suggest about what heaven is like?

Because Muslims believe God will resurrect everyone's body on the Last Day, the dead are not cremated. Every Muslim must be laid in the earth to wait for the Last Day. Destruction of a body by fire is considered wrong.

Heaven and hell

After judgement the good are taken to heaven, **jannah**, where their reward will be closeness to God. Unbelievers and those who have sinned will go to hell, **jahannam**, where they will be punished. The Qur'an explains that the human mind can never really understand what heaven or hell will be like but heaven is portrayed as a garden. Hell is described as a place of intense heat and torture, which some Muslims understand means that evil will be burnt up so it can no longer exist. One of the Islamic names for God is 'the merciful' and Muslims believe that God will forgive those who ask for forgiveness so that only the most determined sinner will go to hell.

FOR RESEARCH

Use a translation of the Qur'an to find out how Jannah, or heaven, is described. Surah 55: 41–68 would be a useful area to look. List four garden images that are used here.

Why do Muslims believe this?

The reason Muslims are convinced about the existence of life after death is because it is clearly stated in the Qur'an and that is the word of God. The sayings of Muhammad, the **Hadith**, also support this. Muslims argue that life after death is perfectly logical. What would be the point of our life on earth if there were not a life after death? They believe life is a test and the way we behave on earth affects our life after death.

The Qur'an says:

On the day the Hour strikes, mankind will scatter apart. Those who have embraced faith and done good works shall rejoice in a fair garden; but those who have disbelieved and denied Our revelations and the life to come, shall be delivered up for punishment. (30: 15–16)

All things shall in the end return to you Lord; that is He who moves to laughter and tears, and He who ordains death and life. (53: 44)

He brings forth the living from the dead, and the dead from the living: He resurrects the earth after its death. Likewise you shall be raised to life. (30: 18)

PATH TO THE TOP

Use some appropriate technical terms to boost your grade. The following are worth learning.

- **akhirah** the Islamic belief in everlasting life after death – the hereafter
- **barzakh** the period of waiting between death and judgement in Islam
- **jahannam** the Islamic name for hell, which means 'the place of fire'
- **jannah** the Islamic name for heaven, which means 'the garden'

ACTIVITIES

1. Make a poster that outlines the Muslim teachings on life after death. Try to include some specialist terms.

2. Write a paragraph explaining how a Muslim's belief in life after death might affect the way he or she lives their life. Include at least two specific examples.

For discussion

'When you are dead, you are dead.' What sort arguments could support this statement? How would a Muslim respond to it? Do you agree with the statement? Why?

AIM

To understand the British law on abortion and different attitudes towards it.

KEY TERM

abortion the removal of a foetus from the womb before it can survive

Figure E Under British law a foetus can be aborted up until 24 weeks into the pregnancy. If a scan reveals that the child is likely to be born severely physically or mentally handicapped doctors may advise parents to abort. What would you do in such a situation? Should issues like this be decided in court?

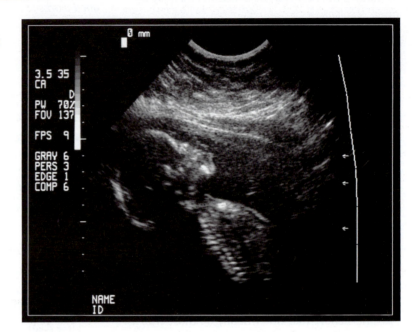

Conjoined twins Jodie and Mary

In 2000, conjoined twins Jodie and Mary became the centre of a legal battle. Against doctors' advice the parents refused to abort the babies and the twins were delivered joined together. Doctors believed they should try to surgically separate them if either child was to stand a chance of survival, but they knew at least one baby would die during the operation. The parents refused, believing it was God's will that their babies were joined. The hospital asked the court to decide. The court ruled that the operation must take place. One baby died. The other has survived and has undergone many operations to rebuild her body. She can now do everything a child of her age would expect to do.

What does the law say about abortion?

In 1967 a law was passed to permit **abortions** in the UK if two doctors agreed that either:

- the mother's life was at risk
- the mother's physical or mental health would suffer
- the child was likely to be born severely physically or mentally handicapped
- there would be a seriously bad effect on other children in the family.

The Act was amended in 1990 to prevent abortions being carried out after 24 weeks of pregnancy. This was because some babies born prematurely after 24 weeks have survived.

ACTIVITIES

1. Were the doctors right to do what they did? Were they acting in the best interests of everyone involved?

2. Create a fact file in your exercise book concerning the British law on abortion.

When does life begin?

Many arguments about abortion hinge on this crucial question. Some people would say a foetus is a life. The reason they give is that the foetus contains everything necessary (the full DNA) to make an individual human being. Once a sperm and an egg fuse a new life begins. That life has the right to exist.

Others disagree, saying that the fusion of a sperm and an egg is no more than a biological reaction, but that at some point during the development of the fertilised egg, life begins. The big question, of course, is when? Is it when the heart begins to beat or when the baby first moves?

Some religions say life begins at the point God puts a soul into the foetus. But when is that? Some people think that a foetus should only be recognised as an independent person when it is capable of surviving outside the mother's body.

ACTIVITY

3. With a partner consider whether any of the arguments above would be affected by advances in medical science such as developments in ultra-sound scans and hi-tech incubators. When would you say life begins? Why?

PATH TO THE TOP

Use appropriate terms to boost your grade. The following is worth learning:

- **doctrine of double effect** the idea that deciding to perform one action can trigger another. For example, a woman might receive treatment for cancer of the womb that, in the process, kills her unborn child. This would not be classed as an abortion because the doctor set out to cure the cancer, not to cause an abortion.

Arguments in favour of abortion

- A woman has the right to choose; it is her body, her life, her future and her child.
- A child's quality of life is important. If a baby is going to lead a miserable life because it is not wanted, or a painful life because of severe disabilities, then it might be kinder to prevent the child ever being born.
- A mother's health and welfare are more important than her unborn child's.
- There are too many people on the planet, and abortion controls population growth.

Arguments against abortion

- Abortion is a form of murder.
- Everyone has the right to be born so they can fulfil their potential.
- All life has value.
- A foetus does have rights and, because it cannot speak for itself, the law must protect it.
- Life is a sacred gift from God and only God can end a pregnancy (see pages 34–7 for more detail on the sanctity of life argument).

ACTIVITY

4. Role-play the discussion between a teenage girl, who wants an abortion because her pregnancy was an accident, and her boyfriend, who believes strongly that abortion is wrong. He wants her to have the baby, which he will look after.

For discussion

'The life of the mother is always worth more than that of her unborn child.' Would you agree with this statement? Are there any exceptions? Is it a mother's right to be free to go out and have a good time or get a better job?

2 Euthanasia

AIM

To understand the British law on euthanasia and the different attitudes towards it.

KEY TERMS

assisted suicide providing a seriously ill person with the means to commit suicide

euthanasia an easy and gentle death

non-voluntary euthanasia ending someone's life painlessly when they are unable to ask, but you have good reason for thinking they would want you to do so, e.g. switching off a life-support machine

voluntary euthanasia the situation where someone dying in pain asks a doctor to end her/his life painlessly

STARTER

Discuss with a partner whether you think a person who is terminally ill has the right to end their life? Is it fair to ask someone else to do it for them?

Euthanasia in Britain

Although it is generally acknowledged that euthanasia is illegal in Britain, there is no specific law forbidding it, but there are laws that forbid murder.

Advances in medical science have brought the issue of euthanasia to the fore because better drugs and more sophisticated machines can prolong life. Some people claim this is not always in the patient's best interests, particularly if their quality of life is poor. There have been several court cases where doctors have requested permission to switch off the life-support machine of a person who is already brain-dead.

ACTIVITY

1. With a partner consider the different forms of euthanasia in the boxes below and decide which ones some people might argue are not actually murder.

Euthanasia

The word comes from the Greek where *eu* = good and *thanasis* = death. Some people refer to euthanasia as 'mercy killing', because it involves ending someone's life painlessly at their request, in order to prevent further suffering.

Voluntary euthanasia

This is also called **assisted suicide** because someone, such as a doctor, deliberately ends a person's life at his or her request. It might be by administering an overdose of drugs or deliberately leaving strong drugs within reach of the patient knowing what they want to do. If the patient subsequently commits suicide then the doctor is considered to have assisted in that suicide.

Passive euthanasia

This is where a patient is allowed to die. A seriously ill cancer patient may not be revived if they collapse from a heart attack or a severely deformed baby is not put on a life-support machine. In some situations a patient may be given strong drugs to control their pain, and these may hasten their death.

Non-voluntary euthanasia

This is when a person helps somebody die without consulting them because the patient is in no position to make their wishes known. The most obvious situation would be switching off the life-support machine of a patient who is 'brain-dead'.

PATH TO THE TOP

Use appropriate terms to boost your grade. The following is worth learning.

- **doctrine of double effect** this involves a doctor treating a person for an illness knowing that the treatment might actually shorten the patient's life. This is not classed as murder

Arguments in favour of euthanasia

- Suicide is legal, so why not help someone who cannot commit suicide themselves.

***Figure F** Diane Pretty, who suffered from a terminal illness, asked the British court's permission for her husband to help her to die because she was in great pain. She did not want him to be prosecuted for murder. When she lost her case she went to the European Court of Human Justice where once again she lost. Do you think that was the correct verdict? Why?*

- If an animal were suffering, we would have it put down because it is the humane thing to do.
- It costs a lot of money to keep people alive when there is no hope for them and that money could be better spent on those who can get better.
- It is their life; they should have the right to end it if they want.
- Someone in great pain has no quality of life, so they should be able to end it in a dignified manner if they wish.
- It is not fair on the relatives to have to watch their loved one dying painfully.

Arguments against euthanasia

- Drugs can be used to control pain.
- Euthanasia is just a fancy name for murder.
- People who ask for euthanasia are often depressed and not in the right state of mind to make such an important decision.
- Some people, like elderly relatives, might be pressured by their family to stop being a nuisance and seek euthanasia.
- Doctors take an oath to save life, it is wrong to ask them to kill people. People would be scared to go to the doctor if euthanasia was an option.
- A doctor's diagnosis can be wrong. People can get better or medical science might find a cure for them.

ACTIVITY

2. Look back to page 23. What connection does Figure A have with the issue on these pages? Would your answer to the question in the activity box on page 23 be any different now?

💬 For discussion

As a class debate this issue 'Euthanasia should be legalised in the UK'. Make a note of the main arguments put forward by each side. Which side do you support and why?

2 The Christian attitude to the sanctity of life

AIM

To understand Christian teachings about the sanctity of life and how these might apply to abortion and euthanasia.

KEY TERM

sanctity of life   the belief that life is holy and belongs to God

The sanctity of life

Christians believe that God created everything and humans were created in God's own image. This makes life holy or sanctified. Christians regard life as a gift from God which they are loaned but do not own. That means they cannot dispose of life as they wish. To emphasize God's special relationship with people, God became human in the person of Jesus. Because Jesus accepted his suffering and never tried to escape from it, Christians believe it teaches them to cherish and preserve life.

The Bible says:

Don't you know that your body is the temple of the Holy Spirit, who lives in you and who was given to you by God? You do not belong to yourselves but to God. (1 Corinthians 6: 19)

God created human beings, making them to be like himself. (Genesis 1: 27)

Let us love one another, because love comes from God. Whoever loves is a child of God and knows God. (1 John 4: 7)

You created every part of me; you put me together in my mother's womb… When my bones were being formed, carefully put together in my mother's womb, when I was growing there in secret, you knew that I was there – you saw me before I was born. The days allotted to me have all been recorded in your book, before any of them ever began. (Psalm 139: 13–17)

Do not commit murder. (1 Exodus 20: 13)

None of us lives for himself only, none of us dies for himself only. If we live, it is for the Lord that we live, and if we die, it is for the Lord that we die. (Romans 14: 7–8)

ACTIVITY

1. Explain in your own words what a Christian understands by the 'sanctity of life'.

The Christian attitude to abortion

Christians agree that taking a life is a sin, but because they do not agree about the moment when life begins, there are differences in their attitudes towards abortion.

- Roman Catholics, and some evangelical Christians, believe life begins at conception, which means abortion is murder. They argue that Christian teachings about the **sanctity of life** mean every human has the right to life and abortion is a serious sin.

- Other Christians believe that life only begins when a foetus can survive independently of its mother. While disliking abortion, they accept that under certain circumstances abortion might be the kindest, most loving thing to do, e.g. when the health of the mother is at stake, or the baby is likely to be handicapped, or the family are too poor to look after another child or the pregnancy was the result of rape. Jesus taught that love is the most important thing.

- Some Christians believe that the decision about abortion should be left to the woman's conscience and that will be directed by God.

The Christian attitude to euthanasia

Christians are agreed that God, the creator of life, is the only one who can end life. This means that euthanasia is a grave sin. Christians differ in their opinions over what medical science should do.

- Some Christians accept that doctors can give drugs to relieve suffering, even if that shortens a patient's life.
- Christians are divided on the issue of switching off life-support machines. Many believe it is acceptable if the patient is already brain-dead.
- Some Christians believe doctors should not carry out expensive treatments that only prolong a poor quality of life but do not aid recovery.
- There are some Christians who say life is precious and everything should be done to prolong it.

The hospice movement

Christians do agree that the hospice movement offers a loving and dignified alternative to euthanasia. Patients who are suffering from an incurable illness can be cared for in a hospice. Cicely Saunders, a Christian who started the movement, totally rejects euthanasia. She says that terminally ill people can have a good quality of life if their pain is controlled and they receive emotional and spiritual support. She is concerned that people should be able to die with dignity.

Figure G *Dame Cicely Saunders, a Christian, founded the first modern hospice in 1967. She said, 'I felt God was tapping me on the shoulder and telling me to get on with the work. I then started to plan the hospice and to raise money in the City. I never gave up hope, I knew it would happen.'*

ACTIVITIES

2. Choose three Bible quotations from page 34 and rewrite them in your own words. Explain what each quotation might teach a Christian about abortion or euthanasia.

3. With a partner, test each other on the meanings of the key terms '**voluntary euthanasia**', '**non-voluntary euthanasia**' and 'assisted suicide'.

4. Make a revision grid to show the Christian attitudes to euthanasia and to abortion. Include a column to list the reasons for these beliefs.

FOR RESEARCH

Find out where your nearest hospice is by visiting www.heinemann.co.uk/hotlinks, typing in the express code 2299P. Alternatively, you could try asking at your public library. Investigate when it was founded and how it is funded? Why might Christians raise money for the hospice?

2 The Muslim attitude to the sanctity of life

AIM

To understand the Muslim teachings about the sanctity of life and how these might apply to abortion and euthanasia.

KEY TERM

sanctity of life the belief that life is holy and belongs to God

The sanctity of life

Muslims believe that because God gives life, God is the only one who can take it away. They believe that life is not theirs to do with as they wish; it is on loan to them from God. Doing anything to harm human life is a serious sin in Islam.

Everyone's lifespan is already set out in God's plan, but nobody knows when their life will end or God's reasons for ending it. Muslims are sure that life is a test which should be accepted without complaint or question. On the final day God will pass judgement on the way each Muslim led his, or her life, and whether he, or she, submitted fully to God's plan.

The Qur'an says:

No one dies unless God permits. The term of every life is fixed. (3: 145)

When their time arrives, not for one hour shall they stay behind: nor can they go before it. (16: 61)

You shall not kill your children for fear of want. We will provide for them and for you. To kill them is a great sin. (17: 31)

Figure H *Abortion concerns most religions. These Muslim women felt so strongly about it that they marched in protest. Are all Muslims against abortion? What arguments would they use to support their views?*

The Hadith says:

The Prophet said, 'In the time before you, a man was wounded. His wounds troubled him so much that he took a knife and cut his wrist to bleed himself to death.' Thereupon God said, 'My slave hurried in the matter of his life therefore he is deprived of the Garden'.

None of you should wish for death for any calamity that befalls you, but should say: 'O God! Cause me to live, so long as life is better for me, and cause me to die when death is better for me'.

He who kills himself with a sword or poison or throws himself off a mountain will be tormented on the Day of Resurrection with that very thing.

Islamic attitude to abortion

Muslims believe that abortion is wrong because the scriptures teach that all life is sacred. It is understood that abortion should not take place once a foetus is completely formed and given a soul. Muslims differ in their interpretation of this.

- Some Muslims will not accept abortion at all because they believe life is a gift from God and the soul was given to a foetus at the moment of conception.
- Others believe that **ensoulment** takes place at 120 days (or 16 weeks) and they are prepared to accept abortion up to that date if it is necessary. Reasons might be that the mother's health is causing concern or that the baby is likely to be physically or mentally disabled.
- Some Muslims accept that abortion may be the lesser of two evils. Losing the life of a foetus may prevent others from suffering. It is not just a mother's physical or mental health that is at stake, abortion could be permitted if the family's welfare was likely to suffer.
- Muslims are generally agreed that a mother's life is always more important than that of her unborn child.

Even if abortion is permitted, however, the Qur'an warns a mother that in the after-life she will have to face her aborted child who will ask why it was killed.

The Muslim response to euthanasia

Muslims believe euthanasia is wrong because it contradicts Islamic teachings on the sanctity of life. No matter how bad the state of the body, Muslims believe the soul is perfect. The reasons for suffering are only known to God, but there is always a purpose because God is never unfair. Everyone, no matter how sick or disabled, should be cared for with love and respect until the end of their natural life. People should show **compassion** to those who are suffering and do everything in their power to relieve their pain. In the after-life Muslims believe they will be judged on the compassion they showed towards others. A person should accept their own suffering as part of God's test. Euthanasia is wrong because it involves altering God's plan for a person's life.

Some Muslims now accept that a doctor can withdraw treatment from a terminally ill patient if the treatment is of no use. This has meant some Muslims would agree to the switching off of a life-support machine because they argue life has already ended.

ACTIVITIES

1. Choose three of the quotations from the sacred texts on these pages and write them in your own words. Against each one write what this teaches Muslims about abortion or euthanasia.

2. Explain what is meant by 'ensoulment'? Why might this affect a Muslim's attitude to abortion?

3. Look at the different Islamic interpretations of the teachings on abortion. Which do you think the women in Figure H might support?

ACTIVITIES

1. Choose either Christianity or Islam and outline what the followers of that religion think will happen when they die. Why do they believe that? How could their beliefs affect the way they live their lives?

2. Make a list of the non-religious arguments in favour of euthanasia and the non-religious arguments against it.

FOR RESEARCH

The parents of the conjoined twins, Jodie and Mary (see page 30), are Roman Catholic. How did their religious beliefs influence their decision about their children? Visit www.heinemann.co.uk/hotlinks, type in the express code 2299P and click on this section to read more about this case.

Tackling an exam question

Here is a **(d)** question from the exam paper.

'Every woman should have the right to an abortion if she wants one.'
Do you agree? Give reasons for your opinion, showing you have considered another point of view. In your answer you should refer to at least one religion. **(4)**

(Edexcel 2004)

The question starts with a statement and the examiner wants you to show that you understand that person's point of view. You need to show that you also understand the opposite side of the argument. You are asked what *you* think so you should explain this in your conclusion. Do not forget that this answer must explain what a Christian or a Muslim would think about the issue. More detailed help with answering a **(d)** question appears on page 123 along with the marking grid for this type of question.

Planning your answer to this question

1. Copy the question into your book and highlight or underline the important words.
2. When you are planning your answer, draw two columns for the different sides of the argument. Check you have put religious evidence into at least one column.
3. Decide what you will say to conclude.

Student's answer

Some people say a woman should be allowed to have an abortion because it is her body after all. She should be able to choose what she wants to do with it. Nobody has the right to tell her what to do. Another reason that she should be allowed to have an abortion is because having a baby might make her ill or even kill her. ✓ (Level 1)

People who disagree with abortions would say a baby is a gift from God. That means it can only be God's decision to take that life away. So they would be against abortion because of their religion. I think a woman should be allowed to have an abortion. After all it is her life, she has got to carry the baby for nine months and she knows what is best for herself and the baby. ✓ (Level 2)

Examiner's comments

This is a Level 2 answer because it is a basic 'for and against' argument. The candidate did not do as the question asked, however, which was to 'refer to at least one religion', so she can only get as far as Level 2. If the student had written, 'Many Muslims believe that abortion is a sin because the Qur'an says people should not kill their children' or 'Some Christians argue that life begins at conception and so abortion is wrong because it is taking a life', then the answer could have gained Level 3. To get to Level 4 the candidate needed to develop both sides of the argument more fully and use them to reach her own conclusion.

Level 1 (1 mark)

For a point of view supported by one relevant reason.

Level 2 (2 marks)

For a basic for and against, or a reasoned opinion, or well argued points of view with no personal opinion.

Level 3 (3 marks)

For a reasoned personal opinion, using religious/moral argument, referring to another point of view.

Level 4 (4 marks)

For a coherent, reasoned personal opinion, using religious/moral argument, evaluating another point of view to reach a personal conclusion.

Student's improved answer

Some people say a woman should be allowed to have an abortion because it is her body and she should be able to choose what she wants to do with it. She has free will; nobody has the right to tell her what to do with her own body. Another reason why she ought to be allowed to have an abortion might be because having a baby could make her ill or even kill her. ✓ (L1)

People who disagree with abortion might say a baby is a gift from God. That means only God can decide to take its life away. Some Muslims are against abortion because they believe in the sanctity of life and because the Qur'an says people should not kill their children. This means they think abortion is a sin. ✓ (L2) *Some Christians would agree with them because they argue life begins at conception so abortion is wrong. Abortion is taking a life and that is forbidden in the Ten Commandments. However, there are Muslims and Christians who say that the life of the mother must take priority over that of her unborn child and abortion would be permitted if the mother's life were at risk.* ✓ (L3)

I think a woman should be allowed to have an abortion under certain circumstances. After all it is her body and she is the one who has to carry the baby for nine months. I do not think it is fair if a girl who has been raped has to go through with an unwanted pregnancy. She would also be reminded of her attacker every time she saw the child. It would ruin her life and it would be a terrible life for a child who was not loved or wanted. ✓ (L4)

2 Putting it all together

3 a) Definition required here (see p. 24).

b) Be clear which group you are talking about. Name them and say what their views are. Try to cover all the views you have learned. Pages 26–7 will help you.

c) Choose Islam and begin your answer 'In Islam...'. Remember to say *what* their views are and *why* they believe that. Look at pages 36–7 for help.

d) This is your chance to give a personal opinion. Say *what* you think and *why*. Then state what people who disagree with you say and why. Pages 30–1 deal with this issue. Remember to give the views of either Christians (see pp. 34–5) or Muslims (see pp. 36–7). Sum up with your conclusion. Page 123 will help you answer this type of question.

SECTION TWO: MATTERS OF LIFE AND DEATH

You must answer ONE question from this section.

EITHER QUESTION 3

3 a) What does *paranormal* mean? **(2)**

b) Outline the different attitudes towards life after death in Christianity. **(6)**

c) Choose **ONE** religion **other than Christianity** and explain why there are different attitudes towards euthanasia in that religion. **(8)**

d) *'Abortion is never the right solution.'*
Do you agree? Give reasons for your opinion, showing you have considered another point of view. In your answer you should refer to at least one religion. **(4)**   Q3

(Total 20 marks)

OR QUESTION 4

4 a) What does *abortion* mean? **(2)**

b) Choose **ONE** religion **other than Christianity** and outline the teachings about abortion in that religion. **(6)**

c) Explain why there are different attitudes towards euthanasia in Christianity. **(8)**

d) *'Near-death experiences are proof of life after death.'*
Do you agree? Give reasons for your opinion, showing that you have considered another point of view. In your answer, you should refer to at least one religion. **(4)**   Q4

(Total 20 marks)

Leave blank

---

4 a) Keep your definition brief (see p. 30).

b) Begin by saying, 'In Islam...' then write the teachings down clearly (see pp. 36–7).

c) You need to state *what* the different Christian attitudes are and, for each one, *why* they believe it. Pages 34–5 will help you with the points, page 122 gives help in writing a **(c)** answer.

d) Your views are requested so you could begin, 'I think... because...'. Then give a different viewpoint. Make sure you have included what a Christian or a Muslim would say about near-death experiences. Consult pages 24–9 and page 123 for help with writing a **(d)** answer. Make sure you conclude with what you think, and why.

3 MARRIAGE AND THE FAMILY

Figure A *A traditional family group.*

Figure B *A single mother with two children from different relationships.*

In this chapter you will learn:

- about the changing attitudes in the UK to cohabitation and marriage
- about the purposes of marriage as expressed in a Christian and a Muslim marriage ceremony
- about the attitudes of Christianity and Islam to sex outside marriage (faithfulness)
- about the attitudes to divorce in the UK
- about the attitudes of Christianity and Islam to divorce (including re-marriage) and the reasons for the attitudes
- about the changing nature of family life (nuclear family, extended family, re-constituted family) in the UK
- about the teachings of Christianity and Islam on family life and its importance
- how churches help with the upbringing of children and keeping the family together
- how the mosque helps with the upbringing of children and keeping the family together.

The key terms you must know are:

cohabitation, marriage, faithfulness, pre-marital sex, promiscuity, adultery, re-marriage, nuclear family, extended family, re-constituted family

ACTIVITIES

1. Study Figures A and B with a partner. Figure A shows a typical family group in the 1950s. Figure B shows a modern-day family group. What do these photographs show you about changes in attitudes towards relationships and family life?

2. As a class, list the advantages and disadvantages of each type of family.

MARRIAGE AND THE FAMILY

AIM

To understand changing attitudes in the UK towards sexual relationships outside marriage.

KEY TERMS

adultery an act of sexual intercourse between a married person and someone other than their marriage partner

cohabitation living together without being married

faithfulness staying with your marriage partner and having sex only with them

marriage the condition of a man and woman legally united for the purpose of living together and, usually, having children

pre-marital sex sex before marriage

promiscuity having sex with a number of partners without commitment

GOALIE CAUGHT 'PLAYING AWAY'

Celebs divorce imminent

'I won't have her back at any price,' says duped husband

DNA test for love rat

'I'll bring my baby up alone,' says top executive

British attitudes towards sexual relationships

If newspapers are anything to go by, the virtue we prize most is **faithfulness**. The celebrity who 'cheats' on his partner is the one who comes in for the most condemnation. For many people it does not matter whether a couple are married to each other or not, what matters is whether trust has been betrayed. If a couple are married and one of them has a sexual affair with somebody outside of the marriage, it is called **adultery**.

There has been a big change in British attitudes towards sexual relationships. In the past couples who had **pre-marital sex** were thought to be immoral and those who cohabited were said to be 'living in sin'. Sex outside of marriage was considered wrong because, since contraception was hard to obtain, there was a high chance a woman would become pregnant and her child would not be born into the traditional family structure. If a couple have sex before they are married it is called

pre-marital sex. This might be a one-night stand or part of a more meaningful relationship.

Cohabitation

Today many couples live together before marrying. This enables them to find out whether they are suited. If they are not, they can split up and avoid a divorce. **Cohabitation** involves setting up home together and enjoying a sexual relationship in the same way as a married couple. The big difference is that there is no legal commitment to each other, although a cohabiting couple may have commitments such as a mortgage or even children.

In English law, cohabiting relationships are recognised as 'common law' marriages, but cohabiting couples have fewer rights than married ones. Some cohabiting couples might choose to marry later if they want to have children. Others see no reason for a legal or religious commitment and continue to cohabit happily for the rest of their lives.

ACTIVITIES

1. List the advantages and disadvantages of cohabitation.

2. Why do you think some people decide to get married when they want to have children?

For discussion

If someone has casual sex with various partners without commitment or love, it is called **promiscuity**. Most people think promiscuity is a bad thing. Why is that?

ACTIVITIES

3. What is the difference between promiscuity and adultery?

4. Why do you think many people say promiscuity is a bad thing but cohabitation is good?

Cohabitation does have its critics

Statistically, unmarried couples who live together are more likely to split up than married couples. That may be because it is easier to walk out over a trivial matter without making as much of an effort to sort things out as a married couple might. Critics also say that living together without proper commitment encourages a casual attitude to the relationship so that neither partner will bother to show much care or consideration to the other. Cohabiting couples might think that if they get bored with their partner, they can move in with someone else.

Some people believe that it is not necessary for couples to live together to find out if they are compatible or not. Couples who have lived together and then marry, still get divorced, so it does not guarantee anything.

Marriage is still very popular

Despite the changing attitude towards sex outside **marriage**, many people still get married. It is not just religious people who choose marriage because there are just as many civil weddings today. Some people even return to get married again after their previous marriage ended. That suggests marriage has something which cohabitation does not.

FOR RESEARCH

Find out more about the legal rights a couple have if they cohabit. How are these different to the rights a married couple have? A good area to look at is the rights married and unmarried couples have in relation to their children.

Divorce

Unfortunately, changing attitudes mean that divorce is more common. It is estimated that one in three marriages now end in divorce. Most people understand that things can go wrong and they think it might be better for all concerned if a couple separate and begin a new life.

For discussion

As a class, discuss what you think of the idea that 'Marriage should not be for life. Couples should take out a contract for five or ten years with an option on renewal'.

ACTIVITIES

5. Why do you think people still want to get married today even though one in three marriages end in divorce?

6. Choose a TV soap and make a list of the types of sexual relationships and family lifestyles it portrays. How close to real life do you think they are? Are any relationships shown to be more successful than others?

Christian marriage

AIM

To understand the nature and purpose of Christian marriage and the marriage ceremony.

KEY TERMS

adultery an act of sexual intercourse between a married person and someone other than their marriage partner

faithfulness staying with your marriage partner and having sex only with them

STARTER

Look carefully at Figure C and note down all the things you can see that you associate with a traditional Christian wedding ceremony. Add any other features which do not appear in the picture but which you think are an essential part of the ceremony. Which features have religious significance and which are simply traditional?

The purpose of Christian marriage

Christians believe marriage is the ideal way for a man and woman to live together in a lifelong relationship. The Bible says, 'For this reason a man will leave his father and mother and unite with his wife, and the two will become one'. (Mark 10: 7–8)

Marriage is a sacred union blessed by God and some Christians believe it can only end with the death of a partner. Faithfulness is part of Christian marriage and the couple promise this in their vows to each other. Adultery is sinful because it breaks the vow of faithfulness that has been made in the presence of God.

Christians do not believe it is essential that they marry. People can remain single as Jesus did, but they should not enter into a sexual relationship with anyone. Nevertheless, marriage is encouraged and particularly marriage to another Christian because it is hoped the couple will have children who will be brought up in the Christian faith.

The Anglican approach to marriage

Read what the Anglican Church says about the purpose of marriage:

It is God's purpose that as husband and wife give themselves to each other in love throughout their lives, they shall be united in that love as Christ is united with his Church. Marriage is given, that husband and wife may comfort and help each other, living faithfully together in need and in plenty, in sorrow and in joy. It is given, that with delight and tenderness, they may know each other in love, and through the joy of their bodily union, may strengthen the unions of their hearts and lives. It is given, that they may have children and be blessed in caring for them, and bringing them up in accordance with God's will, to his praise and glory. (The Alternative Service Book 1980, SPCK, p. 228)

Figure C *A Christian marriage must take place in a church or chapel.*

The Roman Catholic approach to marriage

During a Roman Catholic wedding ceremony the following is said:

*Father you have made the bond of marriage a holy mystery, a symbol of Christ's love for his Church…
In the love of man and wife, God shows us a wonderful reflection of his own eternal love.*
(Geddes & Griffiths, *Christian Belief and Practice: The Roman Catholic Tradition,* Heinemann, 2002)

The couple are also asked, 'Are you ready to accept children lovingly from God, and bring them up according to the law of Christ and his Church?'
(Geddes & Griffiths, *Christian Belief and Practice: The Roman Catholic Tradition,* Heinemann, 2002)

Other approaches to marriage

Others would add that any marriage is a legal contract that protects the rights of each partner and any children born to them. Children of that marriage are recognised as 'legitimate', which gives them rights of inheritance. For some people, marriage is also important because it unites two families.

For discussion

'You shouldn't get married in a church if you don't want children.' What would a Christian say to this? What do you think?

Key features of a Christian marriage ceremony

- The ceremony takes place in a church in the presence of God who is part of the marriage. Members of the congregation are human witnesses. 'I call upon these persons here present to witness that I [Name] do take you [Name] to be my lawful wedded husband/wife.'
- The couple make vows to each other, with God as their witness. 'I [Name] take you [Name] to be my husband/wife. To have and to hold from this day forward; for better, for worse, for richer, for poorer, in sickness and in health, to love and to cherish, till death us do part, according to God's holy law; and this is my solemn vow.'
- The Bible readings and the priest's talk are about Christian marriage.
- There are prayers to ask for God's blessing.
- There is the giving of a ring to symbolise the unending nature of love and the marriage. 'I give you this ring as a sign of our marriage. With my body I honour you, all that I am I give to you, and all that I have I share with you, within the love of God, Father, Son and Holy Spirit.'
(*The Alternative Service Book 1980*, SPCK, p. 292)

ACTIVITIES

1. List the different points made by the Anglican Church regarding the purpose of marriage. Do you think a cohabiting couple could also achieve this? Why?

2. List the additional points that a Roman Catholic marriage ceremony makes about the purpose of marriage.

3. Copy the grid below and fill in the columns using information on these pages. Include anything else you know or can find out about Christian marriage. Check that each feature you have listed has a religious significance for Christians – bridesmaids, confetti and wedding cake are traditional features but are not religious.

Main features of the Christian marriage ceremony	Significance and meaning of these features

Christian attitudes towards sexual relationships

AIM

To understand different Christian attitudes towards sex outside marriage, divorce and re-marriage.

KEY TERMS

re-constituted family where two sets of children (step-brothers and sisters) become one family when their divorced parents marry each other

re-marriage marrying again after being divorced from a previous marriage

Figure D *These teenagers are members of Silver Ring Thing, an organisation who disagree with pre-marital sex. Visit their website at www.heinemann.co.uk/hotlinks to find out more. Type in the express code 2299P and click on this section to access their website.*

Sex outside marriage

There is some variation in the Christian attitudes towards pre-marital sex.

- The Roman Catholic Church says, 'The sexual act must take place exclusively within marriage. Outside marriage it always constitutes a grave sin.' Catechism of the Roman Catholic Church)
- Other more liberal Protestant groups accept cohabitation if it is a prelude to marriage.
- Many Christians do not agree with sex outside marriage because the Bible clearly teaches that it is immoral. The Ten Commandments state 'You shall not commit adultery' (Exodus 20: 14). Jesus added, 'I tell you, anyone who looks at a woman and wants to possess her is guilty of committing adultery with her in his heart.' (Matthew 5: 28)
- St Paul warned early Christians, 'Since you are God's people, it is not right that any matters of sexual immorality or indecency or greed should be mentioned among you.' (Episians 5: 3)
- Today some liberal Christians accept pre-marital sex if a couple are planning to marry.

- Adultery and promiscuity, however, remain totally unacceptable to Christians.

PATH TO THE TOP

Priests in the Roman Catholic Church are not permitted to marry or have sexual relationships. Priests in the Protestant Church are encouraged to marry and have families.

A few Christians choose celibacy, like Jesus did, so they can concentrate on worshipping God without the distractions of family life. **Celibate** means a person who chooses not to marry or have sex.

Divorce

The Bible says:

Jesus said, 'I tell you, then, that any man who divorces his wife for any cause other than her unfaithfulness, commits adultery if he marries some other woman'. (Matthew 19: 9)

Jesus said to them, 'But in the beginning, at the time of creation, "God made them male and female", as the scripture says. "And for this reason a man will leave his father and mother and unite with his wife, and the two will become one." So they are no longer two, but one. No human being then must separate what God has joined together… A man who divorces his wife and marries another woman commits adultery against his wife. In the same way, a woman who divorces her husband and marries another man commits adultery'. (Mark 10: 5–12)

Not all marriages work out and some Christians seek to end them. Because marriage is a legal contract as well as a religious one, all divorces have to be handled by a court of law. However, there is an important religious aspect to Christian marriage and most Christians do not like the idea of breaking their sacred promises.

The Roman Catholic Church does not accept divorce in any form because vows taken for life cannot be broken. If a marriage has broken down totally, the couple can live apart, but they must remain celibate and never enter into a sexual relationship with anyone else. That would be adultery. In a few cases Roman Catholics are permitted to have their marriage annulled which means the marriage is put aside as though it had never taken place. This is not usual and only permitted if the marriage was a forced one, if one of the partners was not of sound mind or if there was no sexual relationship between the couple after their marriage.

Some Orthodox Christians and liberal Protestants will permit divorce if it is the lesser of two evils. Although they do not like the idea of divorce, they agree that more hurt could be caused to those involved in the family (which might include children) if a failed marriage is forced to continue.

Because Jesus taught his followers that love was the most important thing, allowing divorce might be the most loving thing to do in some cases.

ACTIVITIES

1. Which of the Bible passages on these pages would a Protestant use to show that Jesus did permit divorce in some circumstances?

2. What evidence is contained in the Bible passages that could be used by the Roman Catholic Church to show Jesus disapproved of divorce?

Re-marriage

There are different attitudes among Christians to the issue of re-marriage:

- Since the Roman Catholic Church does not permit divorce, there cannot be any **re-marriage.** However, if a person has lost their partner through death, then re-marriage in the Catholic Church is permitted.

- Some Protestant groups who allow divorce will not permit another religious marriage ceremony in church. They argue that once sacred vows have been broken they cannot be taken again. However, there are other Protestants who permit re-marriage in church because they believe God is prepared to forgive sins and let people make a fresh start.

It is not unusual for a couple who re-marry to bring children from a former marriage to the new one. The stepbrothers and stepsisters settle into a new family, as a **re-constituted family**.

ACTIVITY

3. Copy and complete the table below to show the different Christian views on divorce and re-marriage.

	Views on divorce	Views on re-marriage
Roman Catholic		
Orthodox		
Protestant		

3 The Christian family

AIM

To understand the Christian attitude towards family life and the ways in which the Christian church supports families.

KEY TERM

nuclear family mother, father and children living as a unit

STARTER

Make a list of possible reasons for the rise in the number of single parent families in recent years. Pages 42–3 may help you. Do not forget to consider religious as well as non-religious people.

Christianity and family life

The Bible teaches that marriage provides the best environment for children to grow up in, so Christians believe that ideally a child should have both a mother and a father to care for them. Same sex relationships are forbidden in the Bible and most Christians (apart from the most liberal) would also be against same-sex couples adopting a child. The Gospels suggest that Jesus himself belonged to a **nuclear family** and was brought up by his mother and father. There are even references to him having brothers and sisters.

Having children is one of the main purposes of Christian marriage and parents are encouraged to bring up their children in a loving home. Children will be taught right from wrong and learn Christian values.

Not only do the children benefit from this arrangement but it is thought that family units create a stable society because everyone knows how to behave. Having children who are baptized into the Christian community enables the religion to flourish.

How is a child brought up as a Christian?

Soon after birth a baby is taken to church to be baptized and welcomed into the Christian community. The godparents and parents promise to teach the child about their religion and encourage him or her to be confirmed when they are old enough.

Parents do not just teach their children about Christianity, they also show them how to lead a good Christian life by their own example. At home, Christian families are likely to pray and celebrate major festivals, such as Christmas and Easter. The whole family is likely to attend worship in church on Sundays and at festival times. The children may well go to a Sunday school each week to receive further instruction in Christian beliefs.

Care for each other is an important part of Christian family life. Not only do the parents provide love and all the basic necessities for their children, but children are instructed in the Ten Commandments to obey and respect their parents: 'Respect your father and your mother' (Exodus 20: 12). The Old Testament also states that it is every child's duty to look after their parents when they are no longer able to care for themselves.

The Christian community

The local Christian community assists families throughout their life with everything from bringing up their children in a Christian way to providing homes for elderly relatives. At a church there is often not only Sunday School but also a monthly Family Service where children can worship alongside their parents. This service takes account of the needs and interests of the younger members of the community. Festival times such as Christmas take particular note of children's needs in teaching them more about the festival through nativity plays and carol singing.

Some churches run social groups with a strong Christian ethic. Younger children might go to Brownies, Guides, Cubs, Scouts, or Boys' or Girls' Brigade. Christian youth clubs, meanwhile, are popular with teenagers.

For families facing emotional difficulties or financial hardship, help can come from one of the many Christian charities. These might give specialist advice such as marriage guidance or counselling and support at times of bereavement. Others can assist with financial support when illness or redundancy create hardship.

The Children's Society (see Figure E) is a Christian charity that can assist families facing difficulties.

Older members of the family are also helped with special lunches and social clubs. When they can no longer care for themselves, there are residential homes for the elderly run by Christian organisations which can care for them. Methodist Homes for the Aged is one example. It was founded in 1943 and today it cares for 5,500 people in the UK.

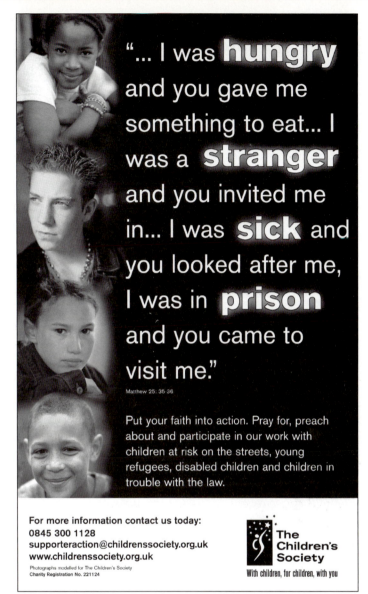

"... I was **hungry** and you gave me something to eat... I was a **stranger** and you invited me in... I was **sick** and you looked after me, I was in **prison** and you came to visit me."

Matthew 25: 35-36

Put your faith into action. Pray for, preach about and participate in our work with children at risk on the streets, young refugees, disabled children and children in trouble with the law.

For more information contact us today:
0845 300 1128
supporteraction@childrenssociety.org.uk
www.childrenssociety.org.uk
Photographs modelled for The Children's Society
Charity Registration No. 221124

The Children's Society
With children, for children, with you

Figure E Why would Christians want to support an organisation like this? Look at the Children's Society's website and find out how their work helps to fulfil the Christian idea of family life. View www.heinemann.co.uk/hotlinks, type in the express code 2299P and click on this section.

ACTIVITIES

1. What is the name for a family that consists of a mother, father and several children?

2. How could Christians fulfil the commandment to care for elderly parents?

3. Make a poster using magazine photographs and words to show how the Church supports families at all stages of life.

FOR RESEARCH

Find out how the Methodist Church cares for elderly people in the UK. What sort of care do they provide? Can they help people in their own homes? Visit www.heinemann.co.uk/hotlinks, type in the express code 2299P and click on this section.

3 Islamic marriage

AIM

To understand the nature and purpose of Muslim marriage and the marriage ceremony.

KEY TERM

faithfulness staying with your marriage partner and having sex only with them

Figure F This jewellery was part of the mahr, or dowry, which a Muslim man paid to his future wife. If the husband divorces his wife in the future, this jewellery remains her property and she can sell it if necessary to finance her new life.

The purpose of marriage in Islam

Marriage is extremely important in Islam; it is the cornerstone of family life. Muslims believe that everyone should marry, have children and raise them as good Muslims. Marriage is God's way of bringing together a man and woman to share love, companionship and sex. Prophet Muhammad married and had children so Muslims follow his example. Faithfulness for life is an important part of an Islamic marriage.

The Qur'an says:

Take in marriage those among you who are single. (24: 32)

By another sign He gave you spouses from among yourselves, that you may live in peace with them, and planted love and kindness in your hearts. (30: 21)

It was He who created you from a single being. From that being He created his mate, so that he might find comfort in her. (7: 189)

Attitudes towards marriage in Islam

Muslims believe that marriage is a social contract that a couple enter into for life, so it should be arranged with care. Because people can easily get swept off their feet by love and make foolish decisions, older experienced members of the family often help in the selection of a partner. Parents search for someone who will be compatible with their son or daughter in as many ways as possible. Introductions and meetings between prospective partners are arranged and the young couple are free to decide whether they like each other enough to meet again, or whether they want to call this particular meeting off. Islam is very clear that no one should forced into a marriage.

There is a religious aspect to marriage in Islam because a Muslim woman can only marry a Muslim man. Ideally a Muslim man should also marry another Muslim, but marriage to a Christian or Jew is permitted because the children will follow the faith of their father (see page 73). At most Muslim weddings the imam will be present and give readings from the Qur'an on the subject of marriage.

Key features of a Muslim marriage ceremony

Muslim wedding ceremonies are essentially very simple.

- The groom agrees a sum of money, the **mahr**, which he will pay to his future wife.
- A contract, the **nikah**, is drawn up between the two who are marrying. The amount of the mahr is specified in it along with any other conditions the woman requests, which might be that her husband has only one wife (see page 53). The groom signs the contract and so does the bride, though she usually asks her father or brother to attend this ceremony and sign on her behalf. The signing of the nikah can take place anywhere: in the home, in a hall or at the mosque. What matters most is that two people witness that the couple have entered into the marriage freely and willingly.
- The imam leads prayers, reads from the Qur'an and gives a talk about marriage.
- Families and friends of the new husband and wife join them in a public celebration of the marriage, a **walimah**. It is only after the walimah that the couple live together.

HINT

Marriage in Islam is to do with signing a contract rather than exchanging vows of love and commitment between husband and wife.

ACTIVITY

1. 'I marry you my daughter according to Allah's Book, the Qur'an and the Sunnah [actions] of the Messenger of Allah (pbuh) and with the dowry agreed upon.'

This is what the father recites when he signs the nikah. Copy it onto your page to form the centre of a spider diagram. Draw 'legs' from it explaining what you think the three underlined parts of this statement mean.

PATH TO THE TOP

Use technical terms to boost your grade. The following are worth learning.

- **mahr** the dowry the groom pays to his future Muslim wife. It shows he respects her as a person in her own right and demonstrates that he can afford to keep a wife and children. Half is usually paid directly to the woman and may take the form of jewellery. The other half may be used to set up home or retained and only paid out in the event of divorce or the husband's death
- **nikah** the Muslim marriage contract. It is essentially a business contract
- **walimah** the Islamic family marriage reception that takes place after the signing of the nikah. This may not take place immediately after the signing of the nikah, but the couple do not usually live together until after the walimah, which is the public part of the wedding

Figure G
A Muslim bride at the walimah.

ACTIVITIES

2. List the four different parts of the Islamic marriage ceremony. Indicate which parts are religious and which are social.

3. With a partner, test your knowledge of the technical terms involved in a Muslim marriage.

3 Islamic attitudes towards sexual relationships

AIM

To understand Muslim teachings about sex inside and outside of marriage and about divorce.

KEY TERMS

adultery an act of sexual intercourse between a married person and someone other than their marriage partner
cohabitation living together without being married
pre-marital sex sex before marriage

Attitudes to sex inside and outside marriage

Muslims are in no doubt that sex must only exist within marriage. Everything else is regarded as adultery and in Islamic countries this carries severe penalties which are set out in the Qur'an. In Islam there can be no pre-marital sex, no cohabitation, no affairs and no adultery.

Not only is sex forbidden outside marriage, it is also haram (forbidden) to behave in a sexual manner. Dressing provocatively is forbidden. Both sexes should dress modestly by wearing baggy clothes which do not reveal the contours of the body and they should cover themselves to the wrist and ankle. Most women also cover their hair when they go out. To avoid temptation, once children reach the age of puberty, they no longer mix freely with members of the opposite sex.

ACTIVITY

1. Prepare a presentation to explain the Muslim attitude to sexual relationships.

Figure H Muslims think it is important to dress modestly and not seek attention by dressing indecently. Muhammad said halal clothing was anything that is suitable for performing prayers. What design of garments would be the most practical and discreet for a woman to wear to perform her prayers? Do you think the clothes you wear say anything about you? What message could tight clothing give about a person? Would a Muslim agree?

Divorce

Muslims accept that, no matter how careful the preparations, not all marriages are successful. Divorce is permitted. In fact the Qur'an says on occasions it may be the right thing to do.

Either keep your wife honestly, or put her away from you with kindness. Do not force a woman to stay with you who wishes to leave. The man who does that only injures himself. (2: 231)

If a woman fears ill-treatment or desertion on the part of her husband, it shall be no offence for them to seek a mutual agreement, for agreement is best. (4: 128)

In the Hadith, Muhammad said, 'Of all things permitted by law, divorce is the most hateful in the sight of God', so although divorce is accepted, it is known that God and Muhammad do not approve of it.

If a marriage runs into difficulties, a Muslim couple should first appeal to their parents who arranged it, to help them overcome their problems. Only if these attempts fail can the husband tell his wife three times, during a three-month period, that he will divorce her. During this time the couple continue to live in the same house, but do not sleep together. At the end of this time, if it is clear that the woman is not pregnant and attempts at reconciliation have failed, the couple are divorced in the eyes of Islam. In the UK a legal divorce is also necessary. The wife's dowry is returned so she is financially independent and can begin a new life. If a woman divorces her husband she gets nothing, although the couple's children must be provided for by their father.

A Muslim who is divorced is free to marry again in exactly the same way as before. Not only is re-marriage permitted in Islam, it is encouraged.

Polygamy

According to the Qur'an:

You may marry other women who seem good to you: two, three or four of them. But if you fear that you cannot maintain equality among them, marry only one. (4: 3)

After the death of his first wife, Prophet Muhammad married again and had many wives. However, the Qur'an restricts the number of wives a man may have at the same time to four. In early times, men were permitted four wives because there was a shortage of young men after wars. It was believed every woman required a man to look after her and she should be given the right to become a mother.

The Qur'an states, however, that a man can only have four wives if he can treat them equally. Some Muslims say that because it is never possible to treat two people exactly the same, it means a man can only have one wife. Other Muslims believe the Qur'an permits up to four wives because it was the practice of Muhammad to have more than one wife. They say it is kinder for a man to take another wife than to divorce his earlier wife, or to have an adulterous relationship. It means there are likely to be less single-parent families if polygamy is permitted. A woman, however, can only have one husband otherwise her children would not know who their father was.

Polygamy is not widely practised among Muslims because it is very expensive to maintain several wives and their families. Most modern Muslims strongly support the idea of a **monogamous** (one wife) relationship and in a non-Islamic country, such as the UK, only the first wife is recognised as a legal wife.

ACTIVITIES

2. Write a short paragraph outlining the Muslim attitude towards divorce. Do not forget to use a quotation to support your points.

3. Explain why some Muslims regard polygamy as acceptable while others do not.

3 The Muslim family

AIM

To understand the Muslim attitude towards family life and the ways in which Islam supports the family.

KEY TERM

extended family children, parents and grandparents/aunts/uncles living as a unit or in close proximity

Family life

- Muslims believe the family unit is one of God's creations and the basis of Islamic society.
- Home is where Muslims learn the essential things in life such as family values, how to look after themselves and how to behave towards other people. Without family units, Muslims believe that society would disintegrate into lawlessness.
- Parents have a responsibility to bring up their children to be good Muslims. This means teaching them about Islam from a young age and setting a good example. Little children are likely to learn stories about the life of Muhammad as well

Figure I *An **extended family** group is one where grandparents, and sometimes aunts and uncles, live in the same house or very close by. This enables members of the older generation to help with childcare and for the family to look after its older members when they are no longer so fit. Many people would say it has a lot to recommend it because everyone is cared for in a loving environment rather than by people paid to do the job.*

as short passages from the Qur'an. They will also be taught how to pray, the correct things to eat, how to dress modestly and how to conduct themselves in public and in private. Their parents will teach them about fasting during Ramadan and encourage them to try a few days at a time.

Caring for everyone

Family life in Islam is a two-way thing. Parents have an obligation to provide for their children until their marriage and that includes assisting them to find a suitable partner. Muhammad said a mother should also be a good friend to her children: affectionate, generous and fair. It is the father's job, meanwhile, to provide for his children to ensure they never have to go without.

In return, Muslim children have a duty to obey and respect their parents all their lives, because no matter how old they are they remain their parents. The Qur'an says that service to God comes first but service to your parents is next in importance.

Your Lord has ordered that you... show kindness to your parents. If either or both of them attain old age in your dwelling, show them no sign of impatience, nor rebuke them; but speak to them kind words. Treat them with humility and tenderness and say, 'Lord be merciful to them. They nursed me when I was an infant'. (17: 23–4)

This means it would be unkind to put an elderly relative into an old people's home where they have to be looked after by strangers. Instead, families should care for elderly relatives in their own home. Many Muslim families live as extended families, which means that older relatives live in close proximity, even in the same house, and are cared for by the younger members of their family.

How the Muslim community helps families

The ummah, the Muslim community, is usually centred on the mosque. Children attend the madrasah (mosque school) for one or two hours after their day at the state school. In the madrasah they learn how to read Arabic and how to recite the Qur'an.

Some boys begin to attend Friday prayers at the mosque with their father during school holidays and at festival times, while at Id the whole family will be likely to attend prayers at the mosque.

The mosque committee is able to provide help for families in crisis. If there are marital difficulties which families are unable to resolve alone, the imam can offer counselling. The family committee at the mosque is also able to help those parents whose children are in trouble with the law. There is also financial help available from the zakah fund at the mosque for families going through times of hardship (see page 109 for more details about zakah).

ACTIVITIES

1. Explain the differences between a nuclear family and an extended family.
2. List the main things that a Muslim child will learn in the home. Which of these do you think is the most important to learn at home?
3. Muhammad said, 'The best of you are those who are kind to your family'. Use this quotation from the Hadith as the centre of a page displaying the different aspects of Muslim family life.
4. 'Religion is what keeps a family together.' What do you think a Muslim would say to this statement? Do you agree?

3 Putting it all together

For discussion

Does it make any difference where a marriage takes place? Does a religious setting create a more serious approach to marriage than a Las Vegas wedding?

ACTIVITIES

1. Write a paragraph explaining why Christians believe marriage is the correct relationship for a man and a woman to live together.

2. With a partner try to work out why some Christians refer to couples who cohabit as 'living in sin'?

3. Outline the ways in which the mosque helps family life.

4. Divide your page into four sections.

- In section one, write down non-religious arguments in favour of cohabitation.
- In section two, write down non-religious arguments against sex before marriage.
- In section three, write down the different Christian attitudes towards sex before marriage.
- In section four, write down the Muslim attitudes towards sex before marriage.

Tackling an exam question

Here is a **(c)** question from the exam paper.

> <u>Explain</u> why there are <u>different attitudes</u> to <u>re-marriage</u> in <u>Christianity</u>. **(8)**
>
> *(Edexcel, 2004)*

Planning your answer to this question

1. Underline the important words in the question. (This has already been done for you in this instance.) You can see there are two parts to this question: firstly, *what* are the different attitudes and, secondly, *why* are there different attitudes? You will have to tackle both aspects if you want to reach the top grades.

2. The important thing to notice in this question is that it says re-marriage not divorce. They are slightly different so be careful!

3. Look back at pages 46–7 in this book if you need to refresh your memory. List the attitudes you are going to include. Write a reason for that attitude against each one. Try to include a specialist term in your answer if possible.

HINT

The **(c)** question carries more marks than any of the other parts of the paper. It is worth 8 marks. The examiner is trying to discover two things. *Do you know the facts* and *do you understand the reasons behind the facts*. The more detail you give, the better the level you will attain.

Student's answer

In Christianity there are different attitudes towards re-marriage. Roman Catholics say you should only get married once. And they mean once, because you aren't allowed to get divorced. The couple have made their vows before God and so they should do their best to remain married and so re-marrying is seen as wrong. ✓ (Level 1) *Protestants on the other hand, are not as concerned about failed marriages so long as both people have got a good reason for splitting up. They are allowed to re-marry so long as the previous marriage ended due to legitimate circumstances.* ✓ (Level 2)

Examiner's comments

The student has reached Level 2, scoring 4 marks. They have given a basic answer that shows they do understand that there are two different Christian responses to re-marriage. However, they have not told the examiner why these reasons are held.

To attain Level 3, the student could have given more detail about the reasons why Protestants allow re-marriage. To reach Level 4, the student needed to show he really understood the differences in Christian attitudes to re-marriage.

Level 1 (2 marks)

For a simple, appropriate and relevant idea.

Level 2 (4 marks)

For a basic explanation showing understanding of a relevant idea.

Level 3 (6 marks)

For a developed explanation showing understanding of the main idea(s) using some specialist vocabulary.

Level 4 (8 marks)

For a comprehensive explanation showing a coherent understanding of the main idea(s) and using specialist language appropriately.

Student's improved answer

In Christianity there are different attitudes towards re-marriage. Roman Catholics say you should only get married once. And they mean once, because you aren't allowed to get divorced. The couple have made their vows before God and so they should do their best to remain married and so re-marrying is seen as wrong. ✓ (L1)

Protestants on the other hand, are not as concerned about failed marriages so long as both people have got a good reason for splitting up. They are allowed to re-marry so long as the previous marriage ended due to legitimate circumstances. ✓ (L2) *Protestants allow re-marriage because they believe God forgives sins and lets people have a second chance.* ✓ (L3)

Although many Protestant churches allow people to get divorced, however, some do not permit re-marriage in church. They say it is impossible to take the same vows again and say you will keep them for life if you have just broken them. ✓ (L4)

5 a) Clear definition required (see p. 42).

b) The answer requires a concise account of the different views Christians hold on this subject. Pages 46–7 will help you.

c) Begin your answer, 'In Islam...' and go on to explain what Muslim family life is like and how that supports the religion (see pp. 54–5). There are two bits to this answer! See page 122 for help with this sort of question.

d) Say what you think about divorce and why. Then say what other people think and why. One of those viewpoints should be clearly linked to Christianity (see pp. 46–7) or Islam (see pp. 52–3). Make sure you come to a conclusion and explain it. Page 123 will help you write this sort of evaluative answer.

Question 5(c) is based on a quesiton in Edexcel Unit A paper 2003. Questions 6(a) and (b) are taken from Edexcel Unit A paper 2004. Question 6(c) is taken from and question 6(d) is based on a question from Edexcel Unit A Specimen Paper.

Leave blank

SECTION THREE: MARRIAGE AND THE FAMILY

You must answer ONE question from this section.

EITHER QUESTION 5

5 a) What is *promiscuity*? **(2)**

b) Outline different Christian attitudes towards sex before marriage. **(6)**

c) Choose **ONE** religion **other than Christianity** and explain why family life is important. **(8)**

d) *'Divorce is bad for everybody.'*
Do you agree? Give reasons for your opinion, showing you have considered another point of view. In your answer you should refer to at least one religion. **(4)**

Q5

(Total 20 marks)

OR QUESTION 6

6 a) What is an *extended family*? **(2)**

b) Choose **ONE** religion **other than Christianity** and outline the teachings about family life in that religion. **(6)**

c) Explain how a Christian marriage ceremony may help a marriage to succeed. **(8)**

d) *'Living together is less of a gamble than marriage.'*
Do you agree? Give reasons for your opinion, showing you have considered another point of view. In your answer you should refer to at least one religion. **(4)**

Q6

(Total 20 marks)

---

6 a) Keep your definition brief (see p. 54).

b) Begin your answer with, 'In Islam...'. Take care with this question which asks for teachings rather than how they are put into practice. Look at pages 54–5, although you might find some help on pages 52–3 as well.

c) There are two parts to this answer. First decide what the key points of the Christian ceremony are, then how each of these helps the marriage succeed. When you write the answer say *what* the point is and then *how* it may help (see pp. 44–5). Page 122 gives help in answering a **(c)** question.

d) You could begin, 'I think... because...'. Give the argument against this, 'Other people think... because...'. Make sure you include one of the religion's views on cohabiting. Make sure you come to a conclusion and explain it. See pages 42–3 for general information, pages 46–7 for the Christian attitude and pages 52–3 for the Muslim attitude. Page 123 deals with how to answer a **(d)** question.

4 SOCIAL HARMONY

In this chapter you will learn:

- about the growth of equal rights for women in the UK and sexism
- about different Christian attitudes to the roles of men and women and the reasons for them
- about the different Muslim attitudes to the roles of men and women and the reasons for them
- about the nature of the UK as a multi-ethnic society including prejudice, discrimination and racism
- about the teachings of Christianity and Islam which promote racial harmony
- about the quality, variety and richness of life in a multi-faith society in the UK, including considerations of religious freedom and religious pluralism
- about the attitudes of Christianity and Islam towards other religions (exclusivism, inclusivism and pluralism) and the reasons for these.

Figure A *This flower is a completely different colour to those around it. Do you find it ugly or beautiful because of this?*

The key terms you must know the meaning of are:

equality, sexism, multi-ethnic society, prejudice, discrimination, racism, racial harmony, multi-faith society, religious freedom, religious pluralism

ACTIVITY

1. Look at Figure A on this page. Why might some people consider it a metaphor for racism or other forms of prejudice? What do you think it might be saying? Look through a few magazines and choose your own image that could form the basis of a poster or article about discrimination. Explain why you chose that picture and how you plan to use it.

4 Sexism

AIM

To understand the growth of women's rights in the UK.

KEY TERMS

equality the state of everyone having equal rights regardless of gender/race/class

discrimination putting prejudice into practice and treating people less favourably because of their race/gender/colour/class

sexism discriminating against people because of their gender (being male or female)

STARTER

Who would you say this poster (Figure B) was aimed at? What are they supposed to do about the situation?

Prepare your daughter for working life.

Give her less pocket money than your son.

After 30 years of equal pay law, women's wages are still 18% lower than men's. www.eoc.org.uk

EQUAL OPPORTUNITIES COMMISSION

Figure B Would you agree? Why?

Women's rights in the twentieth century

Sexual **discrimination** against women has been normal practice throughout history. Because of their greater strength, men have dominated society. However, the past hundred years have seen major challenges and changes to this.

- In 1918, women over 31 years of age received the vote, eighty years after it was given to men.
- In 1928, women over 21 years of age were given the vote and permitted to stand for Parliament.
- The First and Second World Wars made a big impact on women because they were given the opportunity to do responsible jobs and demonstrate their capabilities. This was a big step forward in the campaign for sexual **equality**.
- In 1945, women lost out as men returned from the war and needed their jobs back.
- During the 1950s, the government encouraged married women to give up ideas of a career in favour of being housewives and rearing children.

While a large proportion of women now work, Figure B suggests that the Equal Opportunities Commission thinks there is still a long way to go before the equality is achieved.

Sexism was regarded as common sense. Men with families should take preference over women in the jobs market. Men should earn more money than women because they had families to support. It was also commonly believed that men were more dependable employees than women who were likely to get pregnant and leave their boss in the lurch.

- The arrival of the contraceptive pill in the 1960s challenged that argument. It signalled the rise of feminism. This also marked a wider change in attitudes; people were beginning to think that everyone, no matter what their gender, race or religion, was entitled to the same rights.
- Various laws were passed to enforce that idea, beginning in 1970 with the Equal Pay Act. This gave women the right to the same pay and benefits as a man doing the same job.
- Five years later, the Sex Discrimination Act made it illegal to discriminate against a person based on their gender or marital status. The Act also set up the Equal Opportunities Commission to ensure the legislation was being carried out.

Further progress was made with the 1996 Employment Rights Act. This said people could not be unfairly dismissed for reasons such as being pregnant or taking maternity leave. Today the number of women who work is almost equal to the number of men: the big difference is that a large number of women work part-time. Should this make any difference to their rights?

Equality in education

Today we take it for granted that girls are entitled to the same education as boys and the number of women going to university has been steadily rising. Women have emerged with good degrees equalling, and in some cases exceeding, the achievements of men, which has well and truly defeated the old idea that it is wrong to educate girls. The Victorians had reasoned that because a female brain is smaller than a male one, too much education would cause a woman's brain to overheat!

FOR RESEARCH

As a class, build up a list on the board of:
- things which show women have gained equality during the twentieth century
- evidence of women's increasing equality that you have noticed (e.g. women bus-drivers)
- areas where you think there is still room for improvement (check the Equal Opportunities Commission website for evidence by visiting www.heinemann.co.uk/hotlinks, typing in the express code 2299P and clicking on this section)
- areas where you think men do not have equal rights with women (e.g. types of clothing they are expected to wear).

Per cent

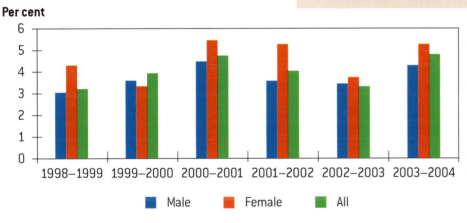

Figure C This graph shows the growth in average weekly earnings of full-time employees in the UK. It allows you to compare the growth experienced by male and female employees.

ACTIVITIES

1. Look at Figure C and other graphs and statistics on the government's website by visiting www.heinemann.co.uk/hotlinks, typing in the express code 2299P and clicking on this section. What do you find the most surprising about women's pay today?

2. With a partner make a list of ten words which could be considered sexist. Here are two to start you off: 'mankind', 'chairman'. Would you say these words are offensive to women or do you think they are used in a fairly neutral way today?

3. Adverts often give a good indication of what is happening in society. Look at some present-day adverts in magazines or on television, and decide whether any are sexist. It is likely that you will be able to find adverts directed against men as well as against women – adverts for new cars are worth studying. Do you think they are harmless fun or sexist? Why?

4 Christianity and the role of women

AIM

To understand different attitudes towards the roles of men and women in Christianity and the reasons for them.

What the Bible says

Today there is a difference of opinion among Christians about the roles men and women should play in the life of the Church and in a Christian family. These different views hinge on interpretations of passages in the Bible.

A *Then the Lord God made the man fall into a deep sleep, and while he was sleeping, he took out one of the man's ribs and closed up the flesh. He formed a woman out of the rib.* (Genesis 2: 21–2)

B *As in all the churches of God's people, the women should keep quiet in the meetings. They are not allowed to speak; as the Jewish Law says, they must not be in charge. If they want to find out about something, they should ask their husbands at home. It is a disgraceful thing for a woman to speak in church.* (Letter of St Paul, 1 Corinthians 14: 33–5)

C *So God created human beings, making them to be like himself. He created them male and female.* (Genesis 1: 27)

D *Jesus travelled through towns and villages, preaching the Good News about the Kingdom of God. The twelve disciples went with him, and so did some women who had been healed of evil spirits and diseases.* (Luke 8: 1–2)

E *Women should learn in silence and all humility. I do not allow them to teach or to have authority over men; they must keep quiet. For Adam was created first, and then Eve. And it was not Adam who was deceived; it was the woman who was deceived and broke God's law. But a woman will*

be saved through having children, if she perseveres in faith and love and holiness, with modesty. (Letter of St Paul, 1 Timothy 2: 11–15)

F *Wives, submit to your husbands as to the Lord. For a husband has authority over his wife just as Christ has authority over the church.* (Letter of St Paul, Ephesians 5: 22–3)

G *So there is no difference between Jews and Gentiles, between slaves and free people, between men and women; you are all one in union with Christ Jesus.* (Letter of St Paul, Galatians 3: 28)

H *At that moment Jesus' disciples returned, and they were greatly surprised to find him talking with a woman. But none of them said to her, 'What do you want?' or asked him, 'Why are you talking with her?'* (John 4: 27)

ACTIVITIES

1. Divide your page into two columns. In one column, note the letter of the quotation and in the column next to it write what you think the passage implies about the role of men or of women.

2. Compare the results of your chart with a partner's. Do you have any differences of opinion?

Those who say men and women should play an equal role in the Christian church argue that Jesus treated women as equals. This would have been particularly unusual in first-century Israel where society was dominated by men. Many of the quotations on this page are by the same author, St Paul. He lived after Jesus and his teaching to the early church shaped the development of Christianity. What do you notice about his attitude towards women in the Church?

How the Christian Church interprets the scriptures

Evangelical Protestants argue that men and women should have different roles in the home and in the church. This group of Christians believes the Bible is the unalterable word of God and should be followed strictly. Their case is based largely on the teachings of St Paul and the fact that Jesus chose twelve male apostles. They believe that:

- women should remain in the home to rear their children and make a Christian home
- women should accept that their husband is superior and do as he wishes
- women should attend church but should take no part in its leadership.

Many Evangelical Protestants believe that the role of the man is to love and provide for his wife and children and to take an active part in worship outside the home. Only men can be church leaders.

The majority of Protestants interpret the scriptures to mean that men and women have equal roles in the church and in the home. Their case is based on what Jesus himself did. There were women with him at the crucifixion and Jesus appeared to women first after the resurrection. They say Jesus only chose male followers because it would have been totally unacceptable in his day to have female disciples. Today, however, they say, it would be wrong to discriminate against women as priests.

Most Roman Catholics believe that men and women have equal roles in life but not in church leadership.

The Lord Jesus chose men to form the college of the twelve apostles, and the apostles did the same when they chose collaborators to succeed them in their ministry … For this reason the ordination of women is not possible. (Catechism of the Roman Catholic Church)

Figure D *When women priests were first ordained into the Church of England in 1994, it caused controversy. Some Christians left the Church of England to become Roman Catholics and even today there are parishes who do not want a woman vicar. Do you think traditional attitudes to the roles of men and women will eventually disappear? What do you think is the most important factor in bringing about that change?*

ACTIVITY

3. Make a fact file of the different Christian attitudes towards the role of men and women in the church.

4 Islam and women's rights

AIM

To understand the different attitudes towards the roles of men and women in Islam and the reasons for them.

STARTER

As a class, debate the following quotation. 'Men and women are different, it's a biological fact! So if they are not the same, then you can never have true equality'.

Sacred writings say:

A *Women shall, with justice, have rights similar to those exercised against them, although men have a status above women.* (Qur'an 2: 229)

B *The search for knowledge is a duty for every Muslim, male or female.* (Hadith)

C *Men have authority over women because God has made the one superior to the other, and because they spend their wealth to maintain them.* (Qur'an 4: 34)

D *O people, your wives have certain rights over you and you have certain rights over them. Treat them well and be kind to them, for they are your partners and committed helpers.* (from Prophet Muhammad's last sermon)

E *Those who surrender themselves to God and accept the true Faith; who are devout, sincere, patient, humble, charitable, and chaste; who fast and are ever mindful of God – on these, both men and women, God will bestow forgiveness and a rich reward.* (Qur'an 33: 35)

F *The best of treasures is a good wife. She is pleasing in her husband's eyes, looks for ways to please him, and takes care of his possessions while he is away; the best of you are those who treat their wives best.* (Hadith)

G *We shall reward the steadfast according to their noblest deeds. Be they men or women, those that embrace the Faith and do what is right, We will surely grant a happy life. We shall reward them according to their noblest deeds.* (Qur'an 16: 97)

H *All people are equal … as the teeth of a comb. No Arab can claim merit over a non-Arab, nor a white over a black person, nor a male over a female.* (Hadith)

PATH TO THE TOP

Try to learn one quotation from the Qu'ran that you could use to justify a point of view about the roles of men and women in Islam.

Figure E Muslim women are not prevented from working, but some families resist the change in traditional family roles. Why do you think they do this? What do you think is the most important reason why attitudes are changing?

ACTIVITIES

1. Divide your page into two columns. In one column, note the letter of the quotation and in the column next to it write what you think the passage implies about the role of men or women.
2. Compare the result of your chart with a partner's. Do you have any differences of opinion?

Equal but different

In accordance with the teachings of the Qur'an and of Prophet Muhammad, Islam says that men and women are equal. Both were created by God and are of equal spiritual worth. They also have an equal right to education, but it would, Muslims argue, be foolish to say that men and women are exactly the same. They clearly are not. Men are physically stronger than women. Women can become pregnant and bear children, which men cannot. So in Islam, men and women have equal rights but different roles and this should ensure that a marriage works and everybody is cared for.

The woman's role

A young woman is expected to marry and have children, which will put her at the heart of the home. It is her duty to care for her husband, to keep a **halal** home and bring up her children to be good Muslims. It is likely that family duties will mean most women have to stay at home while their children are young, but modern Muslims point out that the Qur'an does not forbid a woman from working. Indeed Prophet Muhammad's wife, Khadijah, was a well-respected businesswoman.

Because of family responsibilities, Muslim women are not obliged to attend mosque for prayer. Traditional Muslim women pray at home with their children. More liberal Muslims, however, encourage women to attend mosque and take their part in worship in the women's gallery.

Although men and women worship in separate areas they are praying at the same time and following the same imam. This demonstrates the equality of the sexes in Islam. Similarly women can, and should, go on **Hajj** in just the same way as men. Muslim girls are given the same education as boys at the madrasah and some modern Muslim girls in Britain go to university.

The man's role

A young man is expected to marry and have children. It is his duty to provide for his family, which usually means going out to work. Nevertheless the man has equal responsibility for bringing up his children and ensuring they are taught to become good Muslims. He must ensure his children attend madrasah (see page 55). Many liberal Muslim men help in the home in the same way as the Prophet Muhammad shared the household chores when his first wife worked. Men have a duty to attend mosque to pray and to take their sons with them.

ACTIVITIES

3. After you have read the sections above, make a list of the way traditional Muslim women behave and another list of the way liberal Muslim women may behave. What religious reasons would a liberal Muslim woman give for the differences in her behaviour?
4. In what ways could Prophet Muhammad's wife, Khadijah, be a role model for a modern Muslim woman? Visit the Heinemann website at www.heinemann.co.uk/hotlinks, type in the express code 2299P and click on this section to help you answer this question more fully.

The UK as multi-ethnic society

AIM

To understand the nature of the United Kingdom as a multi-ethnic society.

KEY TERMS

discrimination putting prejudice into practice and treating people less favourably because of their race/gender/colour/class

multi-ethnic society many different races and cultures living together in one society

prejudice believing some people are inferior or superior without even knowing them

racial harmony different races/colours living together happily

racism the belief that some races are superior to others

STARTER

Look at Figures F and G. Work out what the single largest population group in the UK is at present. What percentage of the population belongs to an ethnic minority group? What is the largest ethnic minority group in the UK?

United Kingdom

	Total population		Non-White population
	(Numbers)	(Percentages)	(Percentages)
White	54,153,898	92.1	-
Mixed	677,117	1.2	14.6
Indian	1,053,411	1.8	22.7
Pakistani	747,285	1.3	16.1
Bangladeshi	283,063	0.5	6.1
Other Asian	247,664	0.4	5.3
All Asian or Asian British	2,331,423	4.0	50.3
Black Caribbean	565,876	1.0	12.2
Black African	485,277	0.8	10.5
Black other	97,585	0.2	2.1
All Black or Black British	1,148,738	2.0	24.8
Chinese	247,403	0.4	5.3
Other ethnic groups	230,615	0.4	5.0
All minority ethnic population	4,635,296	7.9	100.0
All population	58,789,194	100	

Figure F The population of the United Kingdom by ethnic group, April 2001.

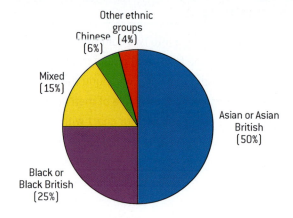

Figure G The non-white population of the UK by ethnic group, April 2001.

Multi-ethnic Britain

Some of the tabloid newspapers use sensational headlines and stories to scare people about the number of 'foreigners' coming into Britain. People already living in the UK become frightened that their life will change for the worse. In reality it is very hard to say what a pure British person is like or even if one exists. History shows that the United Kingdom has continually absorbed people of different nationalities, just like every other country.

A good mix of history

There was an influx of Italians in 54 BC when Julius Caesar and the Romans arrived, then came the Anglo-Saxons from Germany, followed by the Vikings from Scandinavia and the French from Normandy and so it goes on. Many settled, married into families already here and merged into our ancestry.

Since 1066 many other groups both large and small arrived in Britain. Some, like the Huguenots from France and the Jews from eastern Europe, were fleeing religious **prejudice** and persecution. Other people arrived to fill job vacancies when the UK did not have a large enough workforce.

In the nineteenth century Queen Victoria's expansion of the British Empire brought the UK into contact with people from outside Europe. When the Empire became the British Commonwealth, immigrant workers were invited to come from India, Pakistan, Bangladesh, Africa and the Caribbean to undertake the jobs no one else wanted.

At the end of the twentieth century a similar situation happened again. This time people from less prosperous areas such as the former Communist countries of eastern Europe, Iraq, China and other parts of the world arrived as migrant workers or asylum seekers fleeing persecution. They have often been prepared to do poorly-paid jobs in catering and fruit picking that many UK residents do not want to do.

Figure H *Boxer Amir Khan is welcomed back to his home town of Bolton after winning a silver medal in the Athens Olympics in 2004. There was great interest in his Olympic success because no one expected a 17-year-old to do so well. Does his religion or ethnic group matter? Why?*

Racism

Discrimination has been around for a long time and different people have found themselves the victims of it over the years. For example, during the eighteenth century slave traders thought of black people as animals that could be made to work for them. This prevented the traders having a conscience about the way they treated their fellow human beings. Their attitude affected the treatment of anyone who did not look or sound like them. Nowadays, most people agree that **racism** is evil. It creates hatred and can lead to violence such as riots. Violence never solves the problems, it just makes the situation worse.

The 1976 Race Relations Act

This act made it illegal to discriminate against people on grounds of race, colour, nationality, ethnic or national origin, in terms of housing, training, jobs, education or the provision of services. It is illegal to use threatening, abusive or insulting words in public or to publish anything that could stir up racial hatred. The Commission for Racial Equality was also set up to stop race discrimination.

Racial harmony

Too often it is the negative side of a **multi-ethnic society** that makes the news. The advantages of a multi-ethnic society are overlooked.

- The UK has a wide variety of music, culture, food and clothes from the different cultures.
- New ideas arrive in the UK with new people.
- It can make for a more peaceful world as people of different races and nationalities learn to live and work alongside each other.
- It is good for religions to see members of different ethnic groups following their religion.

FOR RESEARCH

Find out the influences that different nationalities or ethnic groups have had on music or fashion.

ACTIVITY

1. Write a reasoned reply to a magazine letter that complains Britain is being weakened by foreigners arriving to live here. Remember to include the benefits that can come from living in a multi-ethnic society.

SOCIAL HARMONY

AIM

To understand the nature of multi faith Britain and evaluate its strengths and weaknesses.

KEY TERMS

multi-faith society many different religions living together in one society
religious freedom the right to practise your religion and change your religion
religious pluralism accepting all religions as having an equal right to coexist

STARTER

The people on this spread belong to an interfaith group. They come from many different religions but are united by their desire to understand each other's religion better and to foster good relations between those religions. What do you think they hope to get out of this? Look at the list of key terms on this page and choose the one you think best describes this group's attitude to other faiths.

Religious freedom

During the twentieth century, Britain has increasingly become a **multi-faith society** and, unlike some parts of the world, religious groups do on the whole exist peacefully side by side in the UK. Although Britain is recognised as a Christian country, there is complete **religious freedom** for people to belong to whatever faith they like, or none at all.

I really look forward to the visits we make, and it's not just the food! However, I do admit to having fond memories of that Jewish social evening we went to; there was a fantastic honey cake Eve made – it was out of this world! We were able to chat to members of the faith about their beliefs and ask questions without fear of causing offence. It was really informative. I never understood about **circumcision** before. You wouldn't normally walk up to a Jew and ask them, would you? But in an informal situation like this we felt we could discuss anything. And actually the Muslims in our group were able to add their comments on circumcision too.

It was great for us. We're a very tiny religion, so it's good to have the chance to tell people what we are about. No, we're not trying to convert anybody, we respect their views. And if you think about it, people who choose to join an interfaith group like this are already happy and confident in their own religion. It's just that we never get many opportunities to explain our philosophies. I think it makes for more peace and tolerance in society if people can get together like this and talk.

Liz is a Roman Catholic.

Paul is a member of the Baha'i faith.

It was our festival of Baisakhi coming up so my community was keen that the interfaith group come and join in. I do not think most of them knew what to expect! We got more from their visit than we expected because of all the questions. It's interesting how some questions really make you think about what you believe. It is so easy to trot out the standard answers, but when someone quizzes you further you have to really consider things. Does it weaken my faith? No, not at all. You could say it strengthens it because it challenges me to think very seriously why I believe something.

The interfaith group does not just go and visit the religion that is having the biggest feast! We also go to people's place of worship and join them for normal worship. No, I do not have any problem with that. God is God as far as I am concerned, whether I join Muslim women in the women's gallery at the mosque or sit in the synagogue I feel I can still join in prayer in my heart. I admit that I do not always know what the words are. My Hebrew is like my Arabic – non-existent! But that's no problem. I really felt we were all joining together to worship God.

Baljinder is a Sikh.

Ann is Christian and a member of the local Salvation Army.

I am all for groups like this. Too often people do not really understand what Muslims believe. I was really pleased when the interfaith group said they wanted to visit the mosque and talk to people. The Muslim community was delighted to welcome them; somebody said afterwards that they did not realise how much we all had in common. Now that's a really positive step, isn't it?

Asma is a Muslim.

ACTIVITIES

1. Read the comments by the interfaith group members and make a list of all the things they have gained from a multi-faith society.

2. Make a list of the difficulties that could arise from living in a multi-faith society.

3. How does the interfaith group attempt to put **religious pluralism** into practice?

4 Christian views on racial harmony and religious freedom

AIM

To understand the attitude of Christians towards other religions and the teachings of Christianity which help to promote racial harmony.

KEY TERMS

multi-ethnic society many different races and cultures living together in one society

prejudice believing some people are inferior or superior without even knowing them

racial harmony different races/colours living together happily

racism the belief that some races are superior to others

What the Bible says:

A *Peter began to speak: 'I now realise that it is true that God treats everyone on the same basis. Those who worship him and do what is right are acceptable to him, no matter what race they belong to'.* (Acts 10: 34–5)

B *Do not ill-treat foreigners who are living in your land.* (Leviticus 19: 33)

C *For God loved the world so much that he gave his only Son, so that everyone who believes in him may not die but have eternal life.* (John 3: 16)

D *You will be doing the right thing if you obey the law of the Kingdom, which is found in the scripture, "Love your neighbour as you love yourself". But if you treat people according to their outward appearance, you are guilty of sin, and the Law condemns you as a law-breaker.* (James 2: 8–9)

E *So there is no difference between Jews and Gentiles, between slaves and free people, between men and women; you are all one in union with Christ Jesus.* (Letter of St Paul, Galatians 3: 28)

F *From one human being he created all races on earth and made them live throughout the whole earth.* (Acts 17: 26)

Figure I *Some people were surprised when the Reverend Dr John Sentamu was appointed Bishop of Birmingham in 2002. Christians, however, should not have had any difficulty accepting his appointment since the Bible makes it clear that prejudice is totally unacceptable.*

ACTIVITY

1. Go through each quotation A–F on page 70 and make a note of what each one teaches Christians about racial issues.

Christianity and racial harmony

The Bible opens with a description of God creating humans in his own image, therefore, Christians believe that everyone should be respected as God's creation. This means prejudice and racism are wrong. There are many more teachings in the Old and the New Testament which reinforce this, for example the story of the Good Samaritan (Luke 10: 25–37). Jesus mixed freely with people of different races as the stories of the Roman centurion's servant (Luke 7: 1–10) and the Samarian woman (John 4: 1–42) show. Jesus' cross was carried by a man from Cyrene in Africa (Luke 23: 26). So, based on Jesus' teachings and example, Christians believe they should work towards **racial harmony**.

The quotation from St Peter **(A)** was spoken after he had a vision of God, so for Christians this is further evidence that they should work towards racial harmony.

ACTIVITY

2. Read the story Jesus told about the Good Samaritan in Luke 10: 25–37. Why do Christians regard this as an important teaching about racism?

The Christian attitude to other religions

Most modern Christians believe that people should be free to follow whatever religion they like, or none at all. There are, however, three different Christian approaches to religious freedom.

Exclusivism: As the word suggests, some people are excluded from heaven. Jesus said, 'I am the way, the truth, and the life; no one goes to the Father except by me' (John 14: 6). Some Christians believe this means only those who follow Christianity will go to heaven. Other religions have gone wrong so it would be right to try to convert a non-believer to Christianity.

Inclusivism: Some Christians believe that while all religions can help people to reach God, only Christianity has the complete answer. This is because Jesus taught that people should believe in him to get to heaven, and only Christians believe in Jesus as the Son of God. This is often the view held by Roman Catholic Christians.

Pluralism: As the word suggests, there are many religions. Some Christians believe that all religions will lead to God, none are superior and none are wrong. People are free to follow the way that suits them best. These Christians do not regard the Bible as 'the word of God', but rather as holy writings like many other sacred books. These Christians do not think they should try to persuade people to change their religion. They say Jesus never tried to convert the Jews in his society and on one occasion he explained to his followers, 'There are many rooms in my Father's house, and I am going to prepare a place for you' (John 14: 2). This is interpreted to mean there are places for people from all religions.

ACTIVITIES

3. Explain the three different Christian approaches to other religions. Be sure to include the reasons for each group's beliefs.
4. What implications do you think these views have for a Christian considering missionary work?

4 Islam and the teachings on racial harmony and religious freedom

AIM

To understand Islamic teachings about other religions and those teachings which help to promote racial harmony.

KEY TERMS

multi-ethnic society many different races and cultures living together in one society
prejudice believing some people are inferior or superior without even knowing them
racial harmony different races/colours living together happily
racism the belief that some races are superior to others

STARTER

Figure J was taken on Hajj. Why do you think Hajj is a good example of the Islamic teachings about racial harmony? One thing you could think about is **ihram**, the clothes worn on Hajj.

What the sacred writings say:

A *All people are equal … as the teeth of a comb. No Arab can claim merit over a non-Arab, nor a white over a black person, nor a male over a female.* (Hadith)

B *Men, We have created you from a male and a female, and made you into nations and tribes, that you might get to know one another.* (Qur'an 49: 13)

C *All God's creatures are His family.* (Hadith)

D *All mankind is from Adam and Eve, an Arab has no superiority over a non-Arab, nor a non-Arab has any superiority over black, nor a black has any superiority over white except by piety and good action. Learn that every Muslim is a brother to every Muslim and that the Muslims constitute one brotherhood.* (from Prophet Muhammad's last sermon)

E *Among His other signs are the creation of the Heavens and the Earth and the diversity of your tongues and colours. Surely there are signs in this for all mankind.* (Qur'an 30: 22)

Look back to page 64 for other scriptural quotations that relate to equality.

Figure J Racial harmony in Islam is shown by Hajj where everyone takes part in the pilgrimage in a spirit of equality and peace.

Racial harmony

Islam teaches that all forms of prejudice are wrong. Muslims believe that racism is sinful because God made everyone on earth so it would be wrong to treat any part of God's creation disrespectfully.

Both the Qur'an and the words of Prophet Muhammad in his final sermon stress the importance of racial harmony. Muhammad demonstrated his belief in the equality of all races when he chose Bilal, a black African Muslim, as his first **muezzin** (prayer caller).

These teachings are put into practice in Islam today. All Muslims belong to the ummah, the brotherhood of Islam, no matter what race, colour or nationality they are. They unite in prayer, shoulder to shoulder, with other Muslims to face Makkah and pray in Arabic. On Hajj everyone is equal as they travel together, obeying the fifth pillar of Islam.

ACTIVITY

1. Explain what Islam teaches about racism. Use evidence from quotations A–E on page 72 to support each of your points.

The Muslim approach to other religions

Islam teaches that everyone is born Muslim, but some people choose to bring their children up in a different religion, or no religion at all. Muslims are taught that everybody has been given free will and no one should be forced to follow a particular religion. Religious pluralism is acceptable to a Muslim because everyone is free to follow the religion of their choice.

Most Muslims, however, believe that Islam is the only correct path to God. They believe that other religions such as Judaism and Christianity were given God's message in the past (in the form of the Torah and the Gospels), but their message became distorted. For this reason, God dictated the Qur'an to Muhammad as the complete and final message to tell humanity how they should lead their lives. Because God gave the message to Jews and Christians in the past, Muslims consider them to be 'people of the book' like themselves. This means a Muslim man is permitted to marry a woman from one of these religions (see page 50).

The Qur'an teaches that those who accept Islam will go to heaven and those who do not will go to hell. For this reason, Muslims believe they have a duty to invite people of other religions to learn about Islam and become Muslim so they can go to heaven along with the believers. Conversion to Islam is a matter for God and the person themselves. The Qur'an is very clear that no one should be forced to convert because that is wrong and meaningless.

Some liberal Muslims believe that Islam is one of several paths to God and for that reason they would accept the validity of other religions.

ACTIVITIES

2. a) What problems do you think a Muslim might experience living in a multi-faith society?
b) Which do you think might cause a Muslim more problems – living in a multi-ethnic society or living in a multi-faith society? Why is that?
3. What is the correct key term for:
a) a society where people of different races live side by side peacefully?
b) treating a person badly when you do not even know them?
c) a society made up of different races?

FOR RESEARCH

Find out more about Hajj and list examples of the ways in which Muslims show equality on the pilgrimage.

4 Putting it all together

ACTIVITIES

1. Design poster showing the different views Christians hold about the role of men and women in the church.

2. In pairs, prepare a presentation showing the different ideas Islam has about the roles of men and women. Make sure you support your comments with evidence.

3. Collect pictures from magazines and newspapers to create a display that illustrates the strengths of a multi-ethnic society.

4. What are the advantages of living in a multi-ethnic society?

5. Test yourself and a partner on the meanings of the key terms on page 59. Write each one on a slip of paper. Look back through this unit of work to find the meaning and write it on a separate slip of paper. In pairs, see how quickly and accurately you can match each word with its meaning.

Tackling an exam question

Here is a **(d)** question from the exam paper.

> *'You shouldn't try to convert people in a multi-faith society.'*
> Do you agree? Give reasons for your opinion showing you have considered another point of view. **(4)**   *(based on Edexcel, 2004)*

Planning your answer to this question

1. The **(d)** question is the evaluation question. It is the only time the examiner asks you what you actually think about an issue.

2. Do not forget that you are also being asked what people who disagree with you will say.

3. Look at page 123 for more help on tackling these **(d)** questions.

Student's answer

I agree. In a multi-faith society people going round trying to convert others to their religion is only going to cause trouble. ✓ (Level 1) *The others might be quite happy with their own religion and do not want any interference. They will say that they will go to heaven if they lead a good life. It's a free world and people ought to be able to believe what they want to. Also it might start fights if people keep pushing their religion at others.* ✓ (Level 2)

Examiner's comments

The student offered her opinion very clearly at the beginning with a reason (Level 1) and she went on to offer other reasons to support it, which took her up to Level 2. But she never told us the other point of view – why some people think you should try to convert people in a multi-faith society. If she had offered that viewpoint her answer might have gone up a level.

Level 1 (1 mark)

For a point of view supported by one relevant reason.

Level 2 (2 marks)

For a basic for and against, or a reasoned opinion, or well argued points of view with no personal opinion.

Level 3 (3 marks)

For a reasoned personal opinion, using religious/moral argument, referring to another point of view.

Level 4 (4 marks)

For a coherent, reasoned personal opinion, using religious/moral argument, evaluating another point of view to reach a personal conclusion.

Student's improved answer

I agree. In a multi-faith society people going round trying to convert others to their religion is only going to cause trouble. ✔ (L1) The others might be quite happy with their own religion and do not want any interference. They will say that they will go to heaven if they lead a good life. It's a free world and people ought to be able to believe what they want to. Also it might start fights if people keep pushing their religion at others. ✔ (L2)

Other people might say you should try to convert people to your religion because it would give them the chance to follow the correct path to God. ✔ (L3) The only problem could be that there are lots of religions in a multi-faith society and if everyone was going round trying to convert people, things could get out of hand. I think it is better if they welcome people who want to learn about their religion, but do not go out searching for converts. ✔ (L4)

4 Putting it all together

7 a) Clear definition required (see p. 68).

b) Take care to answer about different religions not races. You need to briefly discuss the three main approaches (see p. 71).

c) Another what and why question. Begin your answer, 'In Islam...' then say *what* the different attitudes towards men and women's roles are and *why* in the case of Islam. Pages 64–5 will help you. Help with this sort of question is found on page 122.

d) Give your personal opinion and say why you think that. Then give the opposite viewpoint and the reasons for that. Pages 68–9 will give you general help. Be sure you have said what Muslims (see pp. 72–3) or Christians (see pp. 70–1) would say and why. Page 123 will help with this sort of evaluative answer.

Questions 7(b) and 8(c) are taken from the Edexcel Unit A Specimen Paper. Question 8(b) is based on a question from the Edexcel Unit A Specimen Paper.

	Leave blank

SECTION FOUR: SOCIAL HARMONY

You must answer ONE question from this section.

EITHER QUESTION 7

7 a) What is a *multi-faith society*? **(2)**

b) Outline Christian attitudes towards other religions. **(6)**

c) Choose **ONE** religion **other than Christianity** and explain the different attitudes towards the roles of men and women in that religion. **(8)**

d) *'You can't expect people to live together peacefully in a multi-faith society.'* Do you agree? Give reasons for your opinion, showing you have considered another point of view. In your answer you should refer to at least one religion. **(4)**

(Total 20 marks)

Q7

OR QUESTION 8

8 a) What is *prejudice*? **(2)**

b) Choose **ONE** religion **other than Christianity** and outline the teachings of that religion which help to promote racial harmony. **(6)**

c) Explain why there are different attitudes towards the role of men and women among Christians. **(8)**

d) *'A multi-ethnic society is the best way forward for everyone.'* Do you agree? Give reasons for your opinion, showing you have considered another point of view. In your answer you should refer to at least one religion. **(4)**

Q8

(Total 20 marks)

---

8 a) Keep your definition brief (see p. 66).

b) Begin your answer, 'In Islam...' then give a brief account of what Islam teaches about racial harmony (see pp. 72–3).

c) There are two parts to this answer (see pp. 62–3). *What* are the different attitudes and *why*. Page 122 gives help with a **(c)** question.

d) Your views are requested so you could begin, 'I think... because...' Then give the other side's views, 'Other people think... because...' Make sure that you have explained how Christianity (see pp. 70–1) or Islam (see pp. 72–3) would react to this statement. Page 123 will help you answer a **(d)** question.

In this chapter you will learn:

- about the variety and range of specifically religious programmes (religious broadcasts) in terms of general contents and how to assess the reasons for a programme's popularity/unpopularity
- how *either* TV soap operas *or* the national daily press deal with religious and moral issues by studying their handling of one issue in-depth

Figure A *The BBC filming an episode of their popular religious broadcast* Songs of Praise.

- how a specifically religious theme(s) is explored in a film *or* TV drama. This will include an understanding of why the theme is important, how it was dealt with, whether the treatment was fair to religious people and how the treatment of the theme could have been improved
- about the way religion is dealt with in the media in general and how to make a personal evaluation.

Useful concepts

Religious issues involve discussions about life and ultimate questions such as 'Why am I here?' or 'What happens when I die?' which religions may attempt to answer. Alternatively, more straightforward questions to do with the practices of one particular religious group such as 'Can a Muslim marry a divorcee?' or 'Should priests be celibate?' are also considered to be religious issues.

Moral issues are likely to be concerned with whether an action is right or wrong. Although the religions will have something to say about it, people who do not believe in any religion are also likely to have opinions about what is right and wrong. Issues such as abortion and stealing could be considered moral issues. These are also sometimes referred to as ethical issues.

ACTIVITY

1. Go to the BBC's website by visiting www.heinemann.co.uk/hotlinks, typing in the express code 2299P and clicking on this section. Print their 'Religion and Ethics TV and Radio Schedules' for the coming weekend. Analyse the programmes according to:

a) which religion is covered

b) whether the programme is on radio or television, has a worship content, religious news, religious music, moral comment or other relevant material

c) whether you think the coverage of the different religions is balanced or not.

AIM

To understand what the mass media are and the effect they can have on religious and moral issues.

STARTER

With a partner, discuss what is meant by 'the mass media'. Think about:

- who are the mass?
- what are the media?
- how important are the mass media in our society today?
- could the mass media ever be dangerous?

It is easier now to communicate than it has ever been. We can soon discover what is going on in another part of the world and just as quickly let somebody there know our views. Without question we are the best-informed people in history.

The words 'mass media' refer to the many forms of communication we possess, such as radio, television, newspapers and films. The spider diagram on the page opposite illustrates many of these forms.

When someone talks about 'the mass media' the word mass is simply referring to the masses of people who have access to information.

This chapter looks at the way that the media portray religion and religious and moral issues. You have gained a lot of knowledge about Christianity and Islam during your GCSE study so you will be using that knowledge to examine how fair the media are.

How fair is the media?

Most forms of media have another agenda. They are there to make money for the people who own them. The press are there to sell newspapers and magazines and so they are always looking for ways to get us to buy their publications. Films and videos are generally doing the same; they must grab our attention so that we will part with our money. You might think television and radio are different, but they too have to reach large audiences to ensure their survival.

We must watch to see if they have distorted stories to grab our attention, played for a laugh at the expense of the truth, made a scandal out of nothing, or been downright prejudiced in order to boost sales.

***Figure B** How many different forms of communication can you see in this everyday scene?*

TV

Radio

Visual

Audio

Film

Mass Media

Press

Electronic

Newspapers

Magazines

Mobile phones

Internet

ACTIVITIES

1. Draw two columns and in one list the benefits of having so many forms of media. In the other column list the problems and dangers the media create.

2. a) Copy the diagram above. Add any further forms of communication you can think of.

b) Against each form of communication, write the age group you think is most influenced by this type (e.g. 0–9, 10–19, 20–29 etc.).

c) Which form of communication do you think is the most influential? Why?

d) Which would you say is the most trustworthy, and which the least?

e) Which media do you think are most likely to have an impact on a religious or moral issue? Why?

Using the topic for coursework

You may have chosen to deal with this topic as coursework and pages 118–19 will give you specific help on writing your coursework. If you are using 'Religion and the media' as a coursework option,

the following pages will guide you through the way to approach your study of each aspect of the media. Remember that this area of study carries a large proportion of your final mark, so you must give it a great deal of care and attention. You have to write 1500 words, and marks will be awarded for the quality of your written communication in this section as well.

Answering questions on the exam paper

If you are answering questions on the exam paper about 'Religion and the media', the following pages will guide you through the way to approach each aspect of the study. You are free to choose whatever TV programme, newspaper or film that you, or your teacher, thinks best answers the question and is easiest for you to access. Within each area of study, one particular example has been chosen, but it is only there for guidance on how to focus the analysis of your personal choice. Remember that this is the 'Extended Writing' part of the exam paper where you are advised to spend half an hour on an answer. There are only three parts to the questions here but each carries a lot of marks. In addition there are 3 marks at stake for the quality of your written communication.

ACTIVITIES

3. As a class, decide what the word '**propaganda**' means.

4. What has propaganda got to do with the mass media?

For discussion

In pairs, discuss how religion might be involved with propaganda? Do you think it is acceptable for religions to use the media to promote their ideas? What good could it do? What harm could it do?

AIM

To understand the diversity of the national daily press and evaluate the way it handles religious and moral issues.

ACTIVITIES

1. Copy down each headline and write alongside whether it deals with a religious or an ethical issue (or possibly both).

2. Look at the three headlines about Madonna's visit to Israel (one appears in the newspaper extract below). Which do you think is the most neutral of the three? Give reasons for your answer.

Priest in choirboy sex scandal

MADONNA VISITS JEWISH PROPHET'S GRAVE

Pilgrims crushed on Hajj

Singer off key: Madonna in mystical mood dismays strict Jews

Investors urge drug companies to help world's poor

HEAD DRESS BAN FOR MUSLIMS

Vicar steals bishop's wife

Pupils want prayer room in school

It's Madge-ic

MADONNA emerges smiling but teary-eyed from her pilgrimage to a Jerusalem cemetery yesterday.

The star, 46, and hubby Guy Ritchie, 36, joined 2,000 other Kabbalah followers for an emotional ceremony at the grave of mystic Rabbi Yehuda Ashlag.

Madonna, sporting a letter E pendant for her Hebrew name Esther, was guarded by cops as she chanted and prayed. She believes the trip will help wishes come true. Picture: REX

Some people say that nobody reads newspapers today, but with sales of around ten million copies a day that is clearly not the case. Think how quick celebrities and politicians are to sue a newspaper if it prints a story they do not like. Clearly, many people do read newspapers and plenty of people think what they say does matter.

We need to find out how newspapers deal with religious and moral issues. To remind yourself of the difference between a religious issue and a moral or ethical issue, look back to the definitions on page 77.

Newspapers report on real life situations – or do they?

This is where the trouble starts! Generally speaking, newspapers do report on real life events. Unlike soap operas and films, in which characters and their actions are invented by the script writer; the stories in newspapers are true. However, there have been cases of newspapers inventing a story or reporting on something that never happened quite like that. Celebrities and politicians have been upset to find themselves at the heart of a smear campaign based on nothing in particular.

This happens because newspapers have to sell themselves. You have only got to look on a shelf in the supermarket or newsagents to see the number and range of papers for sale. That means that each paper has got to find a way of grabbing people's attention. There will always be the regular readers who buy a copy of the *Sun* as they get off the bus, or have a copy of the *Independent* pushed through their letterbox every morning. But equally there are plenty of people who buy whatever they fancy, or whichever headline catches their attention. That means the headlines must be sensational, sometimes at the expense of the truth.

The in-depth study

You are required to make an in-depth study of the press. The best way to do this is to select a particular day and buy four different newspapers. You can begin your study working in twos or fours, because it is often helpful to discuss your thoughts with others.

Choose:

- one from *The Times,* the *Guardian,* the *Independent* or the *Daily Telegraph.*
- one from the *Daily Mail* or the *Daily Express*
- one from the *Sun* or the *Daily Mirror*
- and one from the same day's evening paper.

This will give you a good range of styles and readership.

- Go through the papers and decide what sort of people are likely to be regular readers of each paper. What is their age, gender, typical type of job?
- Study each paper and briefly note the details of every story that involves religion. Then do the same for each story that involves a moral issue.
- What do you notice about the different papers you studied? Could that fit in with the type of people who read this paper and what might interest or not interest them?
- Select the same four stories that involve a religious or moral issue which appeared in all your papers.
- Design a grid like the one shown in the activity box below so you can compare results. Analyse and record the different treatment the story gets in each paper. Compare the prominence it is given in each paper (buried in the middle or on the front). Compare headlines, pictures, use of language in the main article, how much space is devoted to it. Compare the way the story is handled. Do you think the reporting is fairly neutral, or is it encouraging the reader to think this is a good or a bad thing? (Spend some time on this and pinpoint the evidence that leads you to that conclusion.)

Now use the evidence you have gathered to do the activity.

ACTIVITY

3. Explain how a religious or moral issue has been dealt with in the national daily press.

Story about ....

Newspaper title	Page number in newspaper	Number of column inches	Picture yes/no	Headline	Use of language	How story was handled
A						
B						
C						
D						

5 The soaps

AIM

To understand what a soap opera is and study in-depth the way it handles a religious or moral issue.

STARTER

Everybody talks about watching 'soaps', but what exactly are they? With a partner, make a list of all the TV soaps you can think of. Then try to write a dictionary definition of a soap opera. When you have finished, pool all your answers with members of the class and decide on one definition between you.

The idea for soap operas originally came from America. This kind of serial was aimed mainly at women viewers, so for that reason soap powder manufacturers decided to sponsor them in order to get a good market for their advertising.

Some people are very dismissive of soaps saying, 'I do not watch that sort of thing', but soaps are enormously popular. It is claimed that programmes such as *Coronation Street* can attract an audience of thirteen million viewers each night.

What do we mean by a soap opera?

What makes a soap different from a television play is that it is an ongoing serial which never reaches a conclusion. Different episodes may well be shown three or four times a week, with several storylines running at the same time. There is always the same regular set of characters with guest appearances from other people. The characters live in a small community, often several of them are interrelated and they have to deal with everyday, real-life issues. Viewers get to know the characters well and are interested to watch how they handle the various issues that arise.

HINT

Make sure you are clear what a soap is. Check with your teacher that your choice of study is really a soap. You will lose marks if you answer a question with information about a programme that is not a soap opera. Some examples of soap operas are *Eastenders*, *Coronation Street* and *Emmerdale*. Series such as *Ballykissangel*, *The Vicar of Dibley* and *Holby City* meanwhile, are TV dramas rather than soap operas (see pages 90–1).

Figure C This is a shot from Eastenders. *The photo shows Jane and Ian whose relationship began to develop before the death of Jane's terminally ill husband. Was Jane wrong to have feelings for Ian?*

Why are soaps so popular?

- Soap operas deal with real-life issues and events so they seem relevant to people's lives.
- There is often a helpline number broadcast at the end of the episode so people can get more advice if they need it.
- Soaps show issues from several viewpoints because, as the story unfolds, you see them through the eyes of different characters. This can be helpful in promoting understanding and awareness of an issue.
- Because many people watch soaps, issues get talked about in public. Not only do people chat to each other about the plot at work, at school and at home, but sometimes issues on programmes are discussed on the radio or in magazines.
- Soaps are not frightened of raising some controversial issues that people might be scared to talk about e.g. alcoholism, arranged marriages, teenage pregnancy, incest, homosexuality, terminal illness, a crisis of religious beliefs, euthanasia.
- No matter what difficulties the characters face, good usually triumphs over evil in the stories, so soaps have a feel-good effect on people.

The negative side of soaps

- They are only stories, not real life. Some people get so involved they cannot sort fact from fiction and that can be dangerous. There are magazines devoted to soaps containing interviews with characters, and some newspapers even have updates on the story as though the characters really exist.
- Soap operas can exaggerate everyday life. Lots of things happen to a small group of people. Some viewers forget it is not real and might become dissatisfied, thinking their own lives are boring.
- There is always a crisis, which can portray a false view of reality.

ACTIVITIES

1. Think of one positive and one negative aspect of soaps to add to each of the lists on the left.

2. Choose one soap and watch it regularly for two to four weeks. Write down the name of the soap you are studying. Note all the issues that were raised. Analyse them and categorise them as either moral issues or religious issues (look at page 77 if you cannot remember the difference). Then choose one issue (religious or moral) to base your work on.

- What was the issue?
- Who were the main characters involved in that issue?
- How did the soap deal with it?
- How many different people's views were shown in the soap? Did you think that it was a good rounded view of the problem or was there another aspect they should have shown?
- Why do you think they chose to highlight this issue? Is it topical? Is it an issue people do not find easy to talk about? Would you say a lot of people are faced with this sort of problem? Is it difficult to know the right answer to a situation like this?
- Overall, how well do you think the soap handled this issue? Was it fair in its treatment, or did you feel the soap made it sensational? In what ways do you think it could have been dealt with better?
- You might find useful information for a coursework study on the Internet. Check whether the soap opera you are studying has a website with comments about the storyline or the issues raised. You might find some useful comments on the handling of that issue in a related magazine.

HINT

Focus on the moral or religious issue – not the soap! That means do not get involved in lengthy explanations of the story.

AIM

To understand the variety and range of programmes about religion on television.

Sunday 12 TELEVISION

BBC1	BBC2	ITV1	Channel 4
6.0 Breakfast (T) (S) 92989473 **8.10 Match Of The Day** (T) (S) (R) 8937763 **9.30** Breakfast With Frost (T) (S) 76831 **10.30** The Heaven And Earth Show (S) 59676 **11.30** Countryfile (T) (S) 76218 **12.30** The Politics Show (T) (S) 20164 **1.30 FILM Herbie Goes Bananas** (Vincent J McEveey, 1980) (T) Wonder what Herbie would make of the congestion charge? More car-with-personality adventures starring Cloris Leachman, Charles Martin Smith, John Vernon, Stephen W Burns, Elyssa Davalos, Joaquin Garay, Harvey Korman. 72980 **3.0** EastEnders (T) (S) 33074763 **4.50** Keeping Up Appearances (T) (S) (R) 1303218 **5.20** Points Of View (T) (S) 3416611 **5.35** Songs Of Praise (T) (S) 962701	**6.0 CBeebies:** Teletubbies (T) (S) (R) 2629909 **6.40** The Story Makers (T) (S) (R) 4745367 **7.0 CBBC:** Tom And Jerry Kids (T) (R) 9404270 **7.20** Looney Tunes (T) (R) 6736831 **7.30** Smile (T) (S) 834473 **10.30** Young Indiana Jones Cronicles (T) (S) 8882473 **11.55** Trade Secrets (T) (R) 7761589 **12.05** The Fresh Prince Of Bel-Air (T) (S) (R) 8926386 **12.30** Wildlife On Two (T) (R) 17473 **1.0** The Future Is Wild (T) (S) 46034 **1.30** Sunday Grandstand: (T) (S) Sport Plus 27491928 **1.50** Racing From Goodwood And Longchamps 47207305 **3.30** Cycling 2029473 **4.50** The Big Interview: Tanni Grey-Thompson 1025218 **5.10** Wildlife On Two (T) (S) 8513638 **5.40** Wild (T) (S) (R) 612251 **5.50 FILM The Robe** (Henry Koster, 1953) (T) Bibical drama starring Richard Burton, Jean Simmons, Victor Mature. 29189980	**6.0 GMTV** (T) 3736305 **6.0** News (T) 2231763 **6.10** The Sunday Programme (T) 5364218 **7.30** Diggin' It 4474725 **8.25** Up On The Roof (T) 1505763 **9.25 CITV:** UP2U (T) (S) 8690270 **9.55** How 2 (T) (S) (R) 9238589 **10.10** Finger Tips (T) (S) 9479744 **10.30** The Championship (T) (S) 89102 **11.0** My Favourite Hymns (T) (S) 39744 **12.0** ITV News; (T) (S) Weather 3984034 **12.05** London Today; (T) (S) 3983305 **12.10** F1: Italian Grand Prix (T) (S) 30725928 **3.10** Goodwood Revival (S) 1758909 **4.10** Car Hunt (T) (S) 2006164 **4.40** London Tonight; (T) (S) Weather 1092980 **4.55 FILM Tucker: The Man And His Dream** (Francis Fod Coppola, 1988) (T) (S) Drama in which Jeff Bridges finds big business getting in the way of his car empire. With Joan Allen, Martin Landau, Christian Slater, Frederic Forrest, Mako, Dean Stockwell, Lloyd Bridges. 52969541	**6.15 The Hoobs** Iver Five-O (T) (R) 4232386 **6.40** The Hoobs (T) (R) 8815947 **7.05** Speedway 7342725 **8.0** Racing Rivals 75909 **8.30** Freesport On 4 67980 **9.0 T4** Friends (T) (R) 81560 **9.30** Popworld (T) 2355893 **10.25** Hollyoaks (T) Abby is furious when she hears what's happened to Zara. 95771676 **12.50** Faking It: The T4 Specials (T) Can a history student fake it as a graffiti artist? 9664015 **2.05** The OC (T) The gang head to Palm Springs for some parent-free fun. Not a recipe for disaster or anything. 4419183 **3.05** Collateral: T4 Movie Special (T) Behind the scenes with Tom Cruise, Michael Mann, Jamie Foxx and Jada Pinkett Smith. 9233744 **3.35** Smallville: Superman The Early Years (T) Jonathan gets powered up thanks to Clark's Kryptonian dad. 7715386 **4.35** Stargate SG-1 (T) 7606831 **5.30 Wreck Detectives** (T) Dredging for a 17th century warship. 82218
6.15 Last Of The Summer Wine (T) (S) (R) 190763 **6.45 Antiques Roadshow** Haltwhistle (T) (S) A letter written by JRR Tolkien, fittings from the Titanic's sister ship, and a Roman coin found near Hadrian's Wall. 844560 **7.35 News;** (T) Regional News; Weather 356744		**6.45 ITV News;** (T) (S) Weather 499638 **7.0 Emmerdale** (T) (S) Debbie confesses she is upset that Cain has gone away without telling her. 8725 **7.30 Coronation Street** (T) (S) Things aren't going well for factory girl Kelly. 183	**6.35 Scrapheap Challenge** (T) Glaswegians the Irn Cru take on Bath rickshaw drivers Maximus as they battle to create the best dam-busting machines from junk in just 10 hours. 35812 **7.30 News** Including sport and weather. 725
8.0 Casualty The Ties That Bind Us – Part Two (T) (S) Harry breaks the news that Nina's daring rescue may have devastating consequences. Lucy Benjamin guest stars. 8299 **9.0 PREVIEW Silent Witness** Death by Water – Part One (T) (S) Leo and Harry's professional rivalry erupts following Sam's departure. Tom Ward and William Gaminara star. Continues tomorrow. 1763	**8.0 Get A New Life** Canada (T) (S) Problems emerge as Paul Doody and Toni Syrett attempt to relocate to Canada. 9541 **9.0 Crisis Command: Could You Run The Country?** Flood – One (T) (S) Three contestants are given the chance to run the country during a simulated flooding crisis. Will they heed the advice of Air Marshal Tim Garden, Amanda Platell and retired police and intelligence offficer Charles Shoebridge? 9305	**8.0 Heartbeat** Secrets And Lies (T) (S) Oh dear, there's a blackmailer on the loose. 3367 **9.0 PREVIEW Belonging** (T) (S) Adaptation of Stevie Davies' novel, The Web Of Belonging, starring Brenda Blethyn as dedicated wife Jess whose life is turned upside down when husband Jacob (Kevin Whately) walks out on their marriage. With Rosemary Harris, Anna Massey and Peter Sallis. 6454	**8.0 PREVIEW Funny Already: The History Of Jewish Comedy** (T) Documentary charting the history of Jewish humour, from the vaudeville stage to globally successful sitcoms like Seinfield and Roseanne. 1909 **9.0 Who Got Marc Bolan's Millions?** (T) (R) With only £10,000 to his name when he died, where did all the cash go? His family attempts to find out. 4473
10.0 News; (T) Weather 460367 **10.15 Traffic Cops Special: Under Pressure** (T) (S) (R) Documentary following South Yorkshire's traffic unit. 385803 **11.15 Rosh Hashana: Remembering For The Future** (T) (S) Chief Rabbi Dr Jonathon Sacks delivers his annual message for the Jewish New Year, talking to the fathers of murder victims Damilola Taylor and Daniel Pearl. 677218 **11.40 FILM Carry On Loving** (Gerald Thomas, 1970) (T) Smutty comedy starring Sid James and the team. Weatherview 278676 **1.10 BBC News 24** 52656954	**10.0 Little Britain** (T) (S) (R) More ladylike comedy. 84657 **10.30 Match Of The Day 2** (T) Adrian Chiles reviews the weekend's games with highlights of Tottenham Hotspur and Norwich City. 908015 **11.15 3 Non-Blondes** (T) Hidden-camera comedy show. 461763 **11.45 FILM Dead Ringers** (David Cronenberg, 1988) (T) (S) Thriller starring Jeremy Irons. See Film Choice. 856164 **1.35** Close **2.0** BBC Learning Zone: Workskills Wise At Work: Money Matters 96023 **3.0** Webwise For Business: Using The Internet (T) 24955 **4.0** Improving Skills (T) 41110 **5.0** Workplace Skills (T) 94058	**11.0 ITV Weekend News;** (T) (S) Weather 902541 **11.15 Not Just On Sunday** Politics (T) (S) Melvyn Bragg discusses religion within politics. 465589 **11.44 London Weather** (S) 763909 **11.45 F1: Italian Grand Prix** (S) This afternoon's race at Monza. 419314 **12.45 World Rally Championship** Great Britain (T) (S) 27619 **1.15** Motorsport UK (T) (S) 9614145 **1.40** Building The Dream (T) (R) 3380232 **2.05** Trisha (T) (S) 8389348 **3.0** Today With Des And Mel (T) (S) (R) 5376690 **3.45** World Sport (T) (S) (R) 30139 **4.15** ITV Nightscreen 3254313 **5.30** News 84394	**10.0 FILM Alien Resurrection** (Jean-Pierre Jeunet, 1997) (T) Sigourney Weaver's back as a human/alien clone for the fourth outing. The aliens can swim now too. With Winona Ryder, Dominique Pinon. See Film Choice. 1270 **12.0 FILM The Fan** (Tony Scott, 1996) (T) Thriller starring Robert De Niro as a stalker obsessed with baseball star Wesley Snipes. With Ellen Barkin, John Leguizamo. See Film Choice. 99815481 **2.05 Behind The Crime** (T) 8295955 **3.05** The 9/11 Conspriacies (T) (R) 4517145 **4.05** Avenging Terror (T) (R) 3944042 **5.05** Countdown (T) (R) 3723329 **5.50** Angela Anaconda 9714394

ACTIVITIES

1. Look at the extract from the *Guardian* TV guide on page 84. These were the TV programmes shown on a normal Sunday.

a) Go through them carefully and list the ones that have an obvious religious theme. Some have already been circled to start you off. Note the channel and time the programme was broadcast.

b) List any programme titles that might have some religious content. (Just make a guess from the title.)

c) Sort your list of certainties into three categories: films, religious broadcasts and documentaries.

d) Compare the different channels. Who has the most and least?

e) Look at the times of the broadcasts and suggest what sort of people might be watching them at that time.

f) Which religions are featured in this schedule? Which ones have been omitted? Why do you think the television companies are choosing to feature some and not others?

2. Video *The Heaven and Earth Show*. Watch it and answer the questions below.

a) What date and time was this programme broadcast? How would that affect the type of person likely to watch it?

b) Note the style of presentation. How similar is it to a chat show?

c) Note the topics being discussed. How long did each piece last? What age group/gender would that topic interest? Was the topic a moral one or a religious one?

d) Were any parts of the programme multi-faith or multi-ethnic?

e) Go to the programme's website by visiting www.heinemann.co.uk/hotlinks, typing in the express code 2299P and clicking on this section. Is there any additional material available to support a religious person's interest?

Figure D *Philippa Forrester and Ross Kelly presenting* The Heaven and Earth Show.

f) Who do you think this programme is aimed at? How far do you think it succeeds in capturing that audience?

g) What are the differences between this programme and *Songs of Praise*, which is also a religious broadcast? Which do you think would be the most helpful to a Christian who feels isolated? Why?

3. Look at the schedule for today's TV programmes and compare a typical weekday with last Sunday's viewing. Were there any religious programmes on television during the week? How many were shown on Sunday?

5 Religious broadcasts: Songs of Praise

AIM

To analyse and evaluate the content of Songs of Praise *and consider the reasons for its popularity.*

Songs of Praise

Songs of Praise is such a well-known and popular programme that it is worth a detailed study. You could use it to answer an in-depth question on the exam paper about religious broadcasts, or use it to form the in-depth study as part of your coursework.

Here are some interesting facts about the programme.

- Four *Songs of Praise* presenters have gone on to become bishops.
- The audience for *Songs of Praise* is usually between five and seven million viewers.
- The largest audience was 11.4 million at Christmas in 1988.
- The programme has visited over 1800 different churches, chapels and cathedrals.
- The largest congregation was 60,000 at the Millennium Stadium, Cardiff, on 2 January 2000.
- There have been 182 presenters on *Songs of Praise*.
- The programme is regularly broadcast in the Netherlands, Australia, Canada and South Africa.
- Over the past ten years the programme has visited twenty different countries: Australia, Austria, Barbados, Brazil, Bulgaria, Ireland, France, Germany, the Holy Land, Hong Kong, Israel, Majorca, the Netherlands, Norway, Poland, Romania, South Africa, Spain, USA and Zimbabwe.
- Over 12,500 hymns have been sung on the programme over the last 40 years.

ACTIVITY

1. Watch a video recording of *Songs of Praise* and answer the questions below.

a) What day and time was this broadcast?

b) Who presented it? (Check details of the presenter on *Songs of Praise* website at a later date.)

c) What is the format of the programme? Time the different pieces in the programme so you know how long/how many hymns were sung and how long/how many interviews there were.

d) What sort of topics did the interviews cover? What had religion got to do with them?

e) Make notes on the age group and gender of the people who appeared on the programme. Look at the age and gender of the worshippers. Can you deduce anything about who the programme is aimed at?

f) What do you think regular viewers enjoy about the programme?

g) What might put some viewers off watching *Songs of Praise*?

h) If you know a family member or friend who watches *Songs of Praise* occasionally or regularly, ask them what they like about the programme.

PATH TO THE TOP

The following term is worth learning, using it in the exam may help you boost your grade.

- **worship-type programme** a programme where the viewer can join in at home. They can sing or pray to God in the same way as they would in church. For the viewer, the programme is more than entertainment

FOR RESEARCH

Songs of Praise is described as a worship-type programme. How have the producers of the programme made it easier for people at home to take part? List four types of people who would find a worship-type programme particularly helpful and explain why. Look at the *Songs of Praise* website to see what else they offer Christians. The site can be accessed via www.heinemann.co.uk/hotlinks, typing in the express code 2299P and clicking on this section.

ACTIVITIES

2. Outline the content of *Songs of Praise* and explain why some people might find it interesting. Use the notes you made when you watched *Songs of Praise* at the beginning of this lesson as the basis of your answer.

3. If you were asked by the producer of *Songs of Praise* about plans for a programme in your area, what three interviews would you like him to include? What do you think the programme could do to appeal more to a teenage audience?

4. Compare *Songs of Praise* with a religious broadcast like *The Heaven and Earth Show* to understand why one is a worship-type programme and the other is not.

5. Watch one of the religious broadcasts that is basically a complete church service. If you cannot locate one on television, you could listen to a Sunday morning one on the radio.

a) Make a note of the differences between the full service and a religious broadcast like *Songs of Praise*.

b) Which might be the most helpful to someone considering whether to become a Christian? Why?

c) What would be the disadvantages of the full service for viewers at home?

Figure E Songs of Praise *is the most popular religious programme on television at the moment. It takes four days to record the interviews and outdoor material that will be slotted between the hymn singing. Why do you think this programme is so popular?*

5 TV Documentaries

What is a television documentary?

A documentary is a factual film or programme about a serious subject. It is based on things that have happened. There may be some re-enactments of conversations that people had in the past, with actors playing those parts, but they are scenes and conversations that are known to have taken place. Many of the schools broadcasts that you might watch in RE are short documentaries.

The aim of a documentary is to inform the viewer about an issue. You need to assess how well the documentary informs the viewer and, in particular, whether the information given is fair to all concerned, or whether it is biased.

For your GCSE RE exam you need to study a documentary that has a religious theme. This will provide you with material to answer questions in the section on religious broadcasts.

Everyman

Everyman is a BBC documentary series which covers interesting aspects of religion and beliefs. It is an occasional series and is often supported by a fact sheet which can be downloaded from the Internet. One of their programmes was called 'Mediums: Talking to the Dead', another was called 'Message in a Bottle', which was about the launch of Qibla cola, an Islamic version Coca Cola.

Figure F *The BBC documentary* Everyman *featured the launch of Qibla Cola, an Islamic alternative to Coca Cola.*

Who watches documentaries?

The audience for a religious documentary is perhaps larger than you might think. Research shows that many people who say they are not religious are often interested in religious issues, provided that the religion is dealt with sensitively. They like to watch programmes that investigate both sides of the argument, but leave them to make up their own minds. Viewers also say that they do not like it if it the programme assumes they are Christian just because they live in the United Kingdom. While you are watching keep the agnostic viewer in mind and after you have seen the documentary several times weigh up how satisfied they would have been with the presentation.

HINT

The exam board asks you to study a documentary with a *religious theme*. If you are not sure what that means look again at page 77 and double-check with your teacher.

PATH TO THE TOP

Include some specialist terms that you know or have learned from the programme. It is a good way to gain higher marks.

Make sure you have identified the key arguments that the documentary sets out. Sort them into for and against. Try to learn a couple of each to use in your extended writing and gain those important extra marks.

ACTIVITIES

1. Select your television documentary and video it so you can watch it two or three times. It is surprising how much more you spot on a second or third viewing, and with a difficult non-fiction subject the more detail you include the better.

2. Write down briefly what the subject of the documentary was. For instance, you might put that it was about reincarnation or women becoming nuns. No need for any more detail at this stage.

3. As you watch the programme again, begin to note down the different aspects of the subject which the programme shows. For example, if the subject is reincarnation, the programme might begin with people talking about what happened to them. This can be convincing if the people talking are intelligent and sensible. Then the programme might move on to look at the scientific evidence for this phenomenon which might lead you to think that it is all in the mind. A well-produced programme might well conclude with some new information that throws the subject wide open again. Perhaps there is new scientific evidence emerging that shows everything is not as straightforward as it seems.

4. Look at the different aspects that you have written down and decide for yourself how fair and balanced the material was. Would a religious believer be happy with the way their religion was shown, or did it show them as eccentric and old-fashioned?

5. Who do you think the documentary was aimed at in terms of age group and gender? The timing of the programme and its place in the schedules may give you some clues.

6. How interesting do you think religious people would have found this programme? Offer some evidence to support your view. What about the non-religious viewer? Would they have found the programme sufficiently interesting to watch it through to the end? Again give a reason to support your view.

7. How would you have handled this theme if you had been producing the programme?

8. Plan your own documentary on this subject for a younger age group. Consider if there are any parts of the material that would be unsuitable. Write down four points that you want to get across to viewers. How could you make the subject appealing to younger people.

AIM

To understand how television dramas can deal with a religious theme and evaluate their treatment of that theme.

What is television drama?

A television drama has a fictional storyline. It may be a one-off television play or one episode in a series such as *Ballykissangel* or *Monarch of the Glen*. Television dramas often deal with similar religious issues to soap operas, e.g. divorce, adultery, etc. It is important, however, not to base this coursework or exam answer on a soap opera because that is a separate area of study. Check with your teacher that your chosen programme is suitable.

For this part of the specification you are asked to make a detailed study of how a religious theme is handled in a television drama. The exam board is clear that this must be *a religious theme* (not a moral one). Look back to page 77 to remind yourself what the difference is and check with your teacher that the theme you want to study is suitable.

HINT

Do not automatically assume that comedies such as *The Vicar of Dibley* or *Father Ted* will provide you with the best material to discuss a religious issue. Often it can be hard to get a religious theme out of a comedy with a religious setting, because the producers are actually keen to widen the appeal of their programme by discussing something else. You might well find that a TV play, or one of the institutional dramas such as *Holby City*, *London's Burning* or *The Bill*, will give you more material to work with.

Figure G *Dramas such as* Holby City *often deal with religious themes that you could study. In the scene shown above Kath, a devout Catholic, almost succumbs to her attraction to Father Michael after he reveals to her that he is having problems with his faith. What religious dilemmas does this storyline raise?*

HINT

Do not get carried away telling the story. What the examiner is interested in is the religious theme that the programme tackled, so keep that firmly in your mind.

In an exam answer remember to name the television drama you are writing about. The examiner will not have a clue otherwise and worse than that, your answer will not be able to go above a Level 2.

For discussion

'Television dramas always make fun of religious people.' What do you think of this statement based on the programmes you have studied? Support your answer with some hard evidence.

'Religion is too important to be used in a TV play.' Do you agree? What would people who disagree with you say?

ACTIVITIES

1. Make a list of television dramas you have seen or heard about that have dealt with a religious theme. Put the theme alongside each drama and explain why people might be interested in that subject.

2. Choose the television drama that you want to study, making sure that it has a strong religious theme that you can write about. Video the programme because you will need two to three viewings to get as much out of it as possible.

3. Define the religious theme that is being featured. For example, in 2003 *The Bill* ran a story about a police officer accused of helping a terminally ill friend to die. You need to be very clear what religious theme is under discussion. Ideally, the issue needs to be the main point of the drama. If it is a subsidiary issue you might well find there is not much to write about. In this case, look for another drama!

4. Next you need to flesh out the religious theme by explaining how the characters in the drama are involved with it. Take great care not to get carried away retelling the story. Obviously you do need to tell some of the story in order for the theme to make sense, but try to avoid including characters and parts of the plot that do not affect the religious theme. One way you might start could be, 'In the television drama ... the

theme of ... is dealt with'. Keep firmly in your mind that you are being asked to give a clear and coherent outline of how a religious theme is dealt with in the drama.

5. You need to think about how the issue was depicted in the drama. Was the problem shown from different sides or did you just get one angle on it? Were there any characters in the play who were clearly in favour of the issue? What sort of reasons did they give? Were there others who were obviously on the opposing side? Could you understand their point of view? Which religion was involved? Did you think the drama was fair to both sides in this issue, or did it make one side out to be silly or bad without presenting clear evidence? As you are working through answering these questions do not forget to keep the evidence alongside. It will always be, 'Yes, because in the drama ... happens' or 'No, because in the drama ... happens.'

6. As you consider the drama you have watched, try to think what a person who belongs to that religion might think if they watched it. Would they be offended?

7. Finally, you need to consider how the religious issue could have been handled better. The best answers will always come up with some ideas, even if it was a good programme.

RELIGION AND THE MEDIA

AIM

To analyse the religious theme in a film and evaluate whether the treatment of the religion was fair or not and to consider ways the treatment of the religion could have been handled better.

STARTER

Figure H shows a shot from the film *East is East*. This film deals with the religious and social difficulties experienced by a family of mixed race and religion in the north of England. The Muslim father from Pakistan is married to an English woman and their children have been brought up as Muslims, but find themselves increasingly caught between two cultures and, to some extent, two religions. The film has been called 'a black comedy'. Find out what that term means. (Hint: the word 'black' has nothing to do with skin colour.) What appears to be going on in Figure H? What religious difficulties might this cause?

HINT

Make sure you know the full title of the film you are going to be studying. Also be clear in your mind which religion (or religions) is involved. When you are writing your coursework or exam answer put the film's name down at the beginning of your answer. Make sure you state clearly which religion is being portrayed.

Choosing the film

There are many films you could watch that have religious themes; *East is East* is only one of them. Some other popular choices, which have been released some time ago and so are easy to get hold of on video or DVD, are *Bend it like Beckham*, *Priest* and *Four Weddings and a Funeral*. Choosing one on video or DVD is wise because you will probably need to watch it at least twice.

First viewing

Just enjoy it! You need to understand what the story is about, what the religious themes are and the general impression the whole film makes on you.

- In a couple of sentences sum up the story of the film. Be strict with yourself about only using two sentences. As in an English lesson, it is vital that you develop the ability to sum up a plot.
- Read the two sentences that summarise the plot of *East is East* in the 'Starter' box. When you have seen that film you might like to improve on the brief outline given there.

Second viewing

Now the serious work begins. Have a notepad ready and, if at all possible, be in a position to pause the film at crucial times while you make a few notes.

- Under your outline of the film's plot, write down what the religious theme is. (It is possible in some films, such as *Priest*, that the main story and the religious theme are much the same.) If you are working with *East is East* you might note that the father is doing his best to make his children into good Muslims because that is his religious duty as a Muslim father. Examples of this would be arranging marriages for his children, trying to prevent them from mixing with the opposite sex, making sure the family eat halal food, ensuring each son is circumcised as a baby, and so on.
- Look at the way the religious theme is handled. How does the film producer convey the difficulties or conflicts involved? In the case of *East is East* humour is used to good effect. It is 'black comedy' because although some of the situations are extremely funny and the audience cannot help but laugh, there is a serious and often sad side to it. The contrast between the funny and the sad aspect of a situation is cleverly used by the producer, on occasion, to show two sides of a religious issue.

Figure H *One of the religious dilemmas in the film* East is East *concerns the son's freedom to choose his own girlfriend. He is a Muslim and his father believes that he should therefore marry a Muslim girl selected by the family. Do you think relationships that mix cultures or religions should be avoided? Why?*

- How fair do you think the treatment of the religion is? Here you are looking to see if one side is being shown as 'the baddy' or the one we always laugh at. In the case of *East is East* you should ask yourself if the father is always 'the baddy'. Are there any occasions when you feel sorry for him and can understand what he is trying to do? This is also a film in which you will be looking to see if Islam is portrayed fairly. Are there any incidents in the film that you think are put in just to get a laugh and are unfair?

- When the film is finished and you look back over your notes, try to think of ways in which the treatment of the religious theme could have been improved. What did you think of the film?

HINT

The film you are asked to study for this part of the exam, or for your coursework, must have a *religious* theme rather than a moral one. Check with your teacher if you are unsure whether your choice is acceptable.

ACTIVITIES

1. Describe the religious theme that was presented in the film you watched.

2. Explain why this is an important theme.

3. Do you think the treatment was fair to religious people?

5 Putting it all together

Figure I *This is a scene from the soap opera* Coronation Street *when Katy tells Martin that she is pregnant after coming off the pill behind his back. Their relationship is already controversial because he is so much older than her. What other religious or moral themes has this soap opera dealt with that you could write about in an answer?*

This section of the exam paper is like the coursework section and usually has three parts to the question.

1. The **(a)** part of this question requires a description. In simple terms, the examiner is asking you to say *what* is going on.
2. The **(b)** part of the question requires an explanation, so you are being asked to tell the examiner *why* that is happening.
3. The **(c)** part of this question is the evaluative part. The exam specification, which appears on page 77, states that you will be asked to make a personal evaluation of the way religion is dealt with in the media. That is what question **9 (c)** will be about, although you do not know exactly what you will be asked. Nevertheless, you can prepare yourself well to answer this sort of question.

Trying out your answers

Working with a partner is a really good way of practising your answers to these questions and revising material for the exam. The advantage is that your partner can prompt you with little bits of the question at a time. Often that will stop you from wandering off into just telling the story. People also find it easier to talk their answer through first because it sorts out their thoughts. Writing it up afterwards seems much easier. There is also the advantage of listening to someone else tackle the question. It lets you decide what worked and what could have been improved.

To practise answering **(a)** questions, start with one of you saying: 'Describe how a film, or television drama, handled a religious theme.' You can reply by giving the name of the programme you watched. Then say what religious theme it tackled. That now opens the way for you to describe how that theme was handled. This technique can also be used to practise answering **(b)** and **(c)** questions. One of you asks the other 'Why is that an important theme?' After the answer has been given, the partner asks 'Do you think they treated the theme fairly?' When you have finished you will find that most of what you have said to your partner can be put down on paper and you have worked out a good answer.

Tackling an exam question

Here is a **(c)** question from the exam paper.

> *'The media usually makes religious people out to be old-fashioned and out-of-touch.'*
>
> Do you agree? Give reasons for your answer showing you have considered another point of view. In your answer you should refer to at least one religion. **(8)**

Student's answer

I do not agree with this statement because some television programmes do show the good work religious charities do. I saw a programme on BBC 1 about the work of Christian Aid and it showed how Christians had persuaded people in Africa to give their guns up in exchange for food. ✓ *(L1) The project worked really well because it made the area safer for the inhabitants by getting guns off the streets and at the same time it helped to feed the hungry. The Christians involved in that project were shown to be caring people and very aware of what was going on. I wouldn't have said there was anything old-fashioned or out-of-touch with what they were doing. Far from it.* ✓ *(L2)*

On the other hand, I have seen some programmes where they show a church that is full of old people. That leaves you with the idea that Christians are all past it. That is not fair really because not all church-goers are old and doddery. It is a bit of a stereotype. I think the press, which is another form of the media, is more likely to treat religious people unfairly. ✓ *(L3) The tabloids do not often cover religious topics unless there are some celebs involved, but they are quite keen on commenting on Madonna and her different religious experiments. Because it is Madonna I wouldn't say they make her out to be old-fashioned, but they do tend to report it as though she is a bit out-of-touch.*

Overall, I would say that television documentaries do not make religious people out to be old-fashioned and out-of-touch, but the tabloid press does sometimes. ✓ *(L4)*

Level 1 (2 marks)

For a point of view supported by one relevant reason.

Level 2 (4 marks)

For a basic for and against, or a reasoned opinion, or well argued points of view with no personal opinion.

Level 3 (6 marks)

For a reasoned personal opinion, using religious/moral argument, referring to another point of view.

Level 4 (8 marks)

For a coherent, reasoned personal opinion, using religious/moral argument, evaluating another point of view to reach a personal conclusion.

Examiner's comments

The student's answer is a good one because she has considered both sides of the argument and given good examples relating to religion. It is a coherent and well-balanced argument followed by a personal conclusion. The final reference to the tabloid press was unexpected but clever. This answer would give the Student Level 4, 8 marks.

9 a) Choose your programme carefully. It must not be a soap opera or you will lose all your marks. Keep your focus on how the theme was handled. It has to be a religious theme. Do not tell the story in detail; there are no marks for that.

b) There are two parts to this. Firstly, why is it an important religious theme and, secondly, comment on the fairness of the portrayal.

c) This is your chance to give a personal opinion. Say *what* you think and *why*. Then say what other people think and why. Come to a conclusion. Page 123 gives tips on this type of answer.

The first (a) question and the second (b) question are both based on questions from Edexcel Unit A paper 2004.

SECTION FIVE OPTIONS: EXTENDED WRITING

You must answer ONE question from this section. You are advised to spend 30 minutes on this section. You will be assessed on the Quality of Written Communication in this section.

EXAMPLE QUESTION 9

9 a) Outline how **ONE** film or television drama (**not** a soap opera) dealt with a religious theme. **(4)**

b) Explain why this theme is important and whether the treatment was fair to religious people. **(8)**

c) *'Soap operas deal with real life issues and that is a good thing.'* **OR** *'The national press deals with real life issues and that is a good thing.'*
Do you agree? Give reasons for your opinion, showing you have considered another point of view. **(8)**

(Total 20 marks)

EXAMPLE QUESTION 9

a) Describe the way a religious or moral theme was dealt with in a soap opera or by the national press. **(4)**

b) Choose **ONE** specifically religious programme (religious broadcast) and explain why some people might have found it interesting. **(8)**

c) *'Religious people never get a fair deal in films or dramas.'*
Do you agree? Give reasons for your opinion, showing you have considered another point of view. **(8)**

(Total 20 marks)

Leave blank

Q9

Q9

Remember: Although you are being given a choice of two questions on this page, there is no choice in Section Five, Question 9 on the real exam paper.

9 a) Check the theme you are going to write about fits the question. Look back to page 77 if you are in doubt. Say what the theme is first, then how it was handled.

b) Make sure you have chosen a religious broadcast. Focus on the reasons it is interesting. It is worth mentioning what sort of people would have found it interesting and why.

c) Two sides of an argument are required here. Give some examples. Conclude with your opinion and the reasons for it.

6 RELIGION: WEALTH AND POVERTY

Figure A *This is a scene you could find in any British town. Who's fault do you think it is that this has happened? Who's responsibility is it to do something about it?*

In this chapter you will learn:

- about Christian and Muslim teachings on the possession of wealth, uses and dangers of wealth, stewardship, almsgiving and charity, compassion and justice and the relationship between rich and poor
- about the need for world development in response to the causes, extent and effects of poverty in the world
- about the work of Christian Aid and Muslim Aid in world development and the relief of poverty as well as the reasons for their work
- about the relationship of religion to wealth and poverty and how to evaluate it.

ACTIVITY

1. Write down ten words or phrases Figure A brings to mind. Use some of them to write a response to the person who says, 'Britain is a prosperous society'.

AIM

To understand what world poverty means, the extent and effects of it.

STARTER

With a partner, decide what particular possessions mark somebody out as being richer than you. Would it make any difference if those possessions had been bought on credit?

Who is poor?

We can all think of people who are better off than us; some people are fabulously wealthy so that we look like paupers by comparison. At the same time, we can all think of people in the United Kingdom who are much worse off than us. Figure A on page 97 highlights some of the big divides that exist in our society today.

Some of the people we see on television, fleeing from rebel fighters, arrive in refugee camps with only what they are wearing. Their homes have been destroyed and their families killed. They seem even poorer than the homeless man shown in Figure D on page 102, who probably has at least a few blankets and a carrier bag with some possessions in it. Another person entering the refugee camp with shoes and a bag of items they have salvaged would appear positively rich by comparison. It is all relative – it depends on your own position at the time.

The world picture

The terms used when talking about poverty are relative. Most people consider that in the West we live in **developed countries** because the majority of us have a good standard of living and life expectancy.

At the opposite end of the scale, there are countries where the standard of living is much lower and most of the population struggle to survive. Health and life expectancy in these countries are far below those of people living in developed countries. It is not uncommon for people to be suffering from malnourish or starvation. These countries are called **less economically developed countries**. This term is frequently shortened to LEDCs. These are the poor countries that used to be referred to as 'the Third World'.

In between these two extremes there are **developing countries** which are not as affluent as developed countries, but not as poor as the LEDCs. Some of these countries were previously in the Communist parts of eastern Europe. They are now working towards a more prosperous standard of living for their people. Countries such as Malaysia and Brazil also have developing economies.

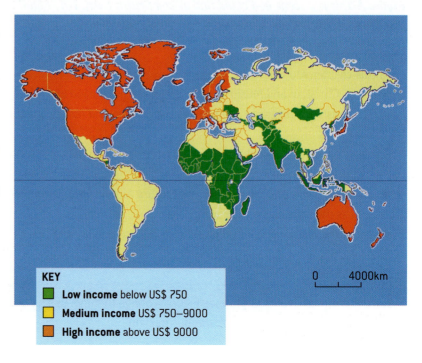

KEY

■ **Low income** below US$ 750
■ **Medium income** US$ 750–9000
■ **High income** above US$ 9000

0   4000km

Figure B This map shows the world divided into countries with low, medium and high domestic incomes.

FACT BOX

- The three richest people on the planet have more wealth than its 600 million poorest inhabitants.
- Eleven million children die every year as a direct result of poverty.
- The richest nations have a one-quarter of the world's population and four-fifths of the world's income.
- Jamaica owes the rich countries the equivalent of £1000 for every man, woman and child on the island. The average wage is £300 a year.

ACTIVITIES

1. Study the map (Figure B) and the fact box. What do you notice about the distribution of wealth and poverty in the world? Estimate the proportion of the world that is developed, developing and less developed. Remember, your total should add up to 100 per cent! Use the information given, along with what you have deduced, to write a press release that could be used by a charity campaigning against world poverty.

2. Visit CAFOD's website by going to www.heinemann.co.uk/hotlinks, typing in the express code 2299P and clicking on this section. Write down four points relating to world poverty you could add to the fact box.

Causes of world poverty

There are many factors that cause poverty and they are not the same in every country. Sometimes one problem will lead to another and things get worse and worse. Here are some of the most common reasons.

- *War:* Conflict often occurs in LEDCs as different groups try to gain power. The conflicts destroy homes and crops and kill innocent people.

Money and food that could have helped people are used to pay for weapons and armies while ordinary people are left homeless and starving.

- *Natural disasters:* Often LEDCs are in areas where floods, earthquakes, hurricanes and other natural disasters are common. These occur and recur, destroying what little economic progress the country has made and adding to the suffering of the population.
- *Debt:* In the past, wealthy nations loaned LEDCs huge sums of money at high interest rates to enable the LEDCs to develop their economies. These deals have resulted in the poorest countries paying the richest countries large amounts of interest. Many LEDCs have been left with debts and mounting interest they will never be able to pay off.
- *Cash crops:* To raise money, LEDCs have been encouraged to use most of their resources to grow crops they can sell to the West such as tobacco, baby vegetables, tea, cotton etc. They grow these instead of growing food to feed their own populations.
- *Lack of health care:* Inadequate medicines, lack of clean water and no proper health education or contraception mean many children die before they are five years old.
- *Corrupt leadership:* Some LEDCs have corrupt governments and corrupt leaders. Aid in terms of money and resources, given to the country by richer nations, is often squandered.
- *Lack of education:* In many LEDCs there is no free education, so there is little chance of poor children being able to go to school and learn how to improve things.

ACTIVITY

3. Which of the points above do you think a charity could help with? List them in order of importance and explain the advantage of tackling them in that order.

6 What is the solution?

AIM

To understand the need for world development and the different types of world aid.

STARTER

As a class decide what is meant by the '**global village**'. Build up a list of things in your classroom that came from another country. Think about the clothing you are wearing, any food in your bag (e.g. bananas, chocolate), the stationery and textbooks you use and so on. Does it matter that 99 per cent of branded trainers are made in Asia, where wages range from 23p to 46p an hour?

It is clear that poverty is a world issue: geographically the problem covers a large area of the globe. Equally, finding solutions to such widespread poverty will require a major input from all the wealthy members of the world.

Some people believe that we should help people in less economically developed countries (LEDCs) because these people are human beings like us. It is simple **justice**. Others argue that we should help people in LEDCs because we depend on them for our survival. If we want the people in these countries to continue growing crops for us, to work in the call-centres that boost our economy and to provide a market where we can sell our goods, then we need to ensure they get enough food to eat.

World development

Because our lifestyle is closely linked to what happens in the rest of the world, the problem of poverty anywhere on the planet concerns us all. Look back at the map on page 98 (Figure B).

ACTIVITY

1. You will notice there is a contrast in the motives behind these two arguments above. Which argument do you think a religious believer would support and why?

Figure C In the summer of 2004, Hurricane Jeanne devastated the Caribbean island of Haiti. Even in normal times, Haiti is one of the poorest countries in the world – 80 per cent of the population are poverty-stricken. The United Nations has developed a food programme there because malnutrition is widespread, with 47 per cent of children under five having stunted growth. The flooding that followed in the wake of the hurricane compounded the country's problems. Nearly 2000 people were killed and the majority of the islanders were left homeless and starving. Why do you think other countries felt the need to help Haiti?

What is the solution to world poverty?

Emergency aid

This involves providing a rapid response to a crisis such as an earthquake or flood where people are likely to die within a short period of time if help does not arrive. Aid agencies have to arrive quickly with food, shelter and medical supplies in order to save people's lives. Assistance may also be needed to dig people out of fallen buildings, bury bodies or get power and water supplies restored.

Long-term development

Once the immediate threat to life has been dealt with, it is important to help an LEDC become self-supporting once more. This could include giving advice and materials to help them improve agriculture so they can feed their population. Other projects might involve setting up schools, hospitals and reliable water supplies. Aid agencies think this money is well spent because it will help the country to get back on its feet and not require charity again.

Education

This is also thought to be an important part of the long-term aid for a country. Education is more than just setting up schools for children. It might include contraceptive advice for women, or advice on nutrition and general hygiene so their children are better looked after and less likely to catch diseases. People are also taught new skills to help them earn a living and become less dependent on charity.

Muslim Aid says:

Whilst responding to emergencies is one of our major priorities, we are also working on strategic programmes for poverty eradication that focus on education, skills training, provision of clean water, healthcare and income generation projects.

CAFOD says:

We believe that all human beings have a right to dignity and respect and that the world's resources are a gift to be shared by all men and women, whatever their race, nationality or religion … We do not just give money to poor communities and walk away, or just support projects in emergencies. We work hand-in-hand with local people to help them to respond to their own real needs. Come rain or shine, we stick with it. Projects like landmine awareness training, farming skills training and water programmes can take years to complete.

ACTIVITIES

2. Look on CAFOD's website by visiting www.heinemann.co.uk/hotlinks, typing in the express code 2299P and clicking on this section. Find one up-to-date example of the emergency aid and one example of long-term aid they are supplying. Why do they think both forms of aid are important?

3. Look at the Islamic Relief website by visiting www.heinemann.co.uk/hotlinks, typing in the express code 2299P and clicking on this section. Find out what emergency aid they are giving at present and what long-term projects they are working on.

4. 'Long term development is more important than emergency aid.' Do you agree? Why?

FOR RESEARCH

One of the causes of world poverty that is listed on page 99 is debt. Research in more detail what this problem involves and what solutions have been suggested. Find out about Jubilee 2000? What success did it have? A good place to start your research would be with their website which can be accessed by visiting www.heinemann.co.uk/hotlinks, typing in the express code 2299P and clicking on this section.

6 Christian teachings about wealth and poverty

AIM

To understand Christian teachings about wealth and poverty.

STARTER

Suggest three possible reasons why the person in Figure D is homeless. One thing is certain, he was not born into it. If a Christian wanted to put biblical teachings into practice, what do you think they could do to help this person?

The Bible says:

A *Rich people who see a brother or sister in need, yet close their hearts against them, cannot claim that they love God.* (1 John 3: 17)

B *Well, religion does make a person very rich, if he is satisfied with what he has. What did we bring into the world? Nothing! What can we take out of the world? Nothing! So then, if we have food and clothes, that should be enough for us. But those who want to get rich fall into temptation and are caught in the trap of many foolish and harmful desires, which pull them down to ruin and destruction. For the love of money is a source of all kinds of evil. Some have been so eager to have it that they have wandered away from the faith and have broken their hearts with many sorrows.* (1 Timothy 6: 6–10)

C *Jesus said, 'You need only one thing. Go and sell all you have and give the money to the poor, and you will have riches in heaven; then come and follow me.'* (Mark 10: 21)

D *My brother and sisters, what good is it for people to say that they have faith if their actions do not prove it? Can that faith save them? Suppose there are brothers or sisters who need clothes and don't have enough to eat. What good is there in your saying to them, 'God bless you! Keep warm and eat well!' – if you don't give them the necessities of life?* (James 2: 14–16)

Figure D *What should the Christian response to this situation be? Why? Which Biblical quotation supports this?*

E *You cannot serve both God and money.*
(Matthew 6: 24)

F *Jesus said, 'Do not store up riches for yourselves here on earth, where moths and rust destroy, and robbers break in and steal. Instead, store up riches for yourselves in heaven, where moths and rust cannot destroy, and robbers cannot break in and steal. For your heart will always be where your riches are.'* (Matthew 6: 19–21)

ACTIVITY

1. Read Bible quotations A–F. Make a note of what each says about being rich. Then decide what implications that might have for a Christian who inherited a fortune from a distant uncle.

What do Christians think about money?

From quotations A–F it might appear at first that Christians think money is a bad thing, but that is not true. Christians believe that God made the world and everything in it, so money cannot be a bad thing. In fact they would argue that wealth is a gift from God to be used for the benefit of others. Money is not the problem, but how you use it might be. Sometimes money makes people greedy and distracts them from helping those around them. Greed may even lead some people to worship money not God. Essentially, most Christians have no problem with the idea of earning money, indeed they believe people should take responsibility for themselves. However, money should be earned in an honest way and not by exploiting others.

Give it all up!

There are a small number of Christians who take Jesus' advice to the rich young man (quote F), which was to go and sell everything, become poor and follow Jesus.

CASE STUDY: MOTHER TERESA

Mother Teresa, who died in 1997, was an example of a Christian who gave up all her possessions to serve God. She trained as a nun before going to India to teach. She saw so much poverty there that she left the convent, learned basic medical skills and went to live and work amongst the poor. 'I felt that God wanted something more from me,' she said. 'He wanted me to be poor and to love Him in the distressing disguise of the poorest of the poor.' Mother Teresa did such exceptional work for 40 years that she is likely to be made a saint.

FOR RESEARCH

Find out more about the work of the Missionaries of Charity which Mother Teresa set up. What centres are there in the UK?

There are a larger proportion of Christians, however, who can see no advantage in making themselves poor and dependent on others. Instead they use some of their wealth to help the less fortunate, but keep enough to provide for themselves and their families. Christians believe that God will judge them on the way they used their wealth to help the poor. For them it as a matter of justice that everyone should receive the basic necessities in life.

ACTIVITIES

2. With a partner, decide on four jobs that would be unacceptable to a Christian because they involve exploiting people?

3. Would most Christians condemn a person for being rich? What does the Bible say are the dangers of being rich?

4. What does the Bible teach is the correct use of money?

6 Putting Christian teachings into practice

AIM

To understand how some Christians put Jesus' teachings about wealth and poverty into practice and to understand the Christian approach to almsgiving and charity.

Jesus said: 'Love your neighbour as you love yourself' (Matthew 22: 39). This sums up the Christian attitude towards people in poverty. Jesus taught his followers to show compassion towards the less fortunate and that means doing more than just feeling sorry for them. It means doing something positive to help.

Jesus also taught that the poor were special to him and their suffering would be rewarded in heaven. 'Happy are you poor; the Kingdom of God is yours' (Luke 6: 20). He went on to point out that the lifestyle of the rich, who had stood by whilst the poor suffered, would be turned upside down. 'How terrible for you who are full now; you will go hungry' (Luke 6: 25).

💬 For discussion

'Charity begins at home.' What is meant by this statement? What would be the advantages of this approach to poverty? Where would it fail? Is this a Christian response to the problem of poverty?

Figure E The Salvation Army, a Christian denomination, collects money to fund many projects to help the poor. They run soup kitchens to feed the homeless, trace missing relatives, work in prison, provide hostel accommodation for the homeless and give support to families in difficulties and to elderly people.

Giving money

Most Christians believe they should donate money to help the poor and some Christians give 10 per cent of their income to the church. A tithe, as it is called, is the amount specified in the Old Testament. Today it is more usual for Christians to put a sum of money in the collection plate that is passed round the congregation during Sunday worship. This is in accordance with St Paul's advice to the Corinthians when he wrote, 'Every Sunday each of you must put aside some money, in proportion to what you have earned' (1 Corinthians 16: 2).

Christians might also give money to charities of their choice. Some may make regular donations, others respond to collections that are being made in the street or to special appeals on television. Giving money to charity is also called **almsgiving**.

Giving time

Showing Christian compassion does not necessarily mean giving money. Some people give their time to help the poor. Mother Teresa was a well-known example of a person who gave her time, indeed she gave her whole life to helping the poor, but she never had any money to donate.

Other things Christians might do include:

- assisting with the preparation and serving of Christmas dinners to the homeless
- working voluntarily in a charity shop
- sorting through donations of food and clothing for a disaster appeal.

PATH TO THE TOP

Use some appropriate terms to boost your grade. The following are worth learning.

- **compassion** understanding the suffering of people and doing something to help them
- **justice** the idea that everyone has the right to be treated fairly. Everyone has the right to have a decent standard of living because everyone is part of God's creation, all life is sacred and people are equal members of the worldwide family of humanity. It is morally wrong to ignore people's problems, people have a duty to help those worse off than themselves
- **stewardship** taking care of something that does not belong to you and using it wisely. Christians believe that all wealth belongs to God and is given to people to use wisely

Christian charities

There are many specifically Christian organisations that have been set up to help the poor. Although they are Christian, they are committed to helping everyone whatever their faith. Some well-known Christian charities include Tearfund, CAFOD and Christian Aid, but there are many less well-known ones such as ABCD (which

stands for Action around Bethlehem for Children with Disabilities). ABCD assists families with disabled children in the Bethlehem area.

CAFOD

CAFOD (The Catholic Association For Overseas Development) explains its vision as follows:

Drawing its inspiration from Scripture, the Church's social teaching, and the experiences and hopes of the poor – those women and girls, boys and men who are deprived, marginalized, or in any way oppressed – CAFOD looks forward to a world in which:

- *the good things of creation are cherished, developed and shared by all*
- *the rights and dignity of each person are respected, discrimination is ended and all are gathered into a single human family from which no-one is excluded*
- *the voice of the poor is heard and heeded by all, and lives are no longer dominated by greed*
- *all have access to food, shelter and clean water; to a livelihood, health and education.*

For discussion

Look at CAFOD's logo. What does the strapline tell us about it's work?

ACTIVITIES

1. Choose one of Jesus' teachings about poverty given on page 104 and explain how a Christian could put it into practice.

2. What could a poor Christian do to help others?

3. 'Justice not charity is the solution to world poverty.' In pairs, decide what you think this means. Then decide whether or not you agree.

RELIGION: WEALTH AND POVERTY

AIM

To understand the link between Christian teachings and the work of Christian Aid in their attempts to remove the causes of poverty.

Christian Aid
We believe in life before death

As part of your coursework, or for your final exam, you are required to make a detailed study of the work of one religious agency involved in working for world development and the relief of poverty. If you are studying Christianity, you could examine the work of CAFOD, Tearfund or Christian Aid. We have chosen to focus on Christian Aid. Access their website by visiting www.heinemann.co.uk/hotlinks, typing in the express code 2299P and clicking on this section. You could choose a different charity if you have access to good material or know a person who works closely with that charity, but make sure that it is a religious charity to qualify for this unit of work.

○ For discussion

Look at Figure F. With a partner discuss what sort of things Christians could do in a situation like this. Why should they get involved?

FOR RESEARCH

Choose one of the many projects Christian Aid is currently involved in and find out more details. Here are some projects you might consider:

- landmine awareness training
- working with AIDS orphans
- feeding the starving in Sudan
- providing help for small businesses in Tajikistan (one of the poorest countries in the world)
- providing education for girls in Afghanistan.

You could look on the Christian Aid website, check with the school library and with the RE department to see whether they have copies of Christian Aid News or write to Christian Aid (with an SAE) requesting a copy. Their address is on page 136.

Figure F This is a scene in Darfur in Sudan where Christian Aid is working to bring relief to the thousands who have been forced from their homes by warring groups. The United Nations said the situation in Darfur was 'the worst humanitarian crisis in the world'.

For discussion

An organisation's logo and strap line can be very revealing. Look at Christian Aid's logo on page 106. What do you think the charity is trying to show by the red symbol in the centre? Their strap line is thought-provoking because it is the opposite of what you would have expected a Christian to say. You have only to look back to Chapter 2, pages 26–7, and the work that you did there to understand that. What is Christian Aid trying to say about its work? Compare this strapline with CAFOD's strapline on page 105.

CASE STUDY: CHRISTIAN AID IN THE SUDAN

Fighting in the Darfur region of the Sudan has killed thousands of innocent people and forced more than a million from their homes. Those who have escaped have ended up in makeshift camps and are still vulnerable to attacks. Christian Aid reported, 'These people are in dire need and supplies of water are desperately short. The rainy season has started, the risk of malaria has increased and many families are without food, shelter, mosquito nets or proper sanitation. If the already short supplies of clean drinking water become contaminated, many people – especially children – will die.'

Christian Aid is responding by supporting the work of church groups and other charities in Sudan. They are providing shelter, water, sanitation and basic sleeping and kitchen materials for 500,000 homeless people. It is also providing extra food for 50,000 children under five and education for school-aged children.

(*Christian Aid News*, summer 2004, p.4)

ACTIVITY

1. Use the material in the case study, along with any more information you can get from Christian Aid's website, its newsletter or newspaper reports on the Internet, to make a leaflet about Christian Aid's work in Darfur. Make sure you explain why Christians should be concerned.

The in-depth study

- Find out when the organisation was founded and what happened that started things off. In the case of Christian Aid you will be looking at the aftermath of the Second World War and a need Christians felt they should respond to.
- Christian Aid regards itself as a Christian organisation and that is not just because the word is in its name. Find out how the Christian Church were involved in setting it up and what role it plays today. The other even more important area to look at is what aspects of Christian teachings about wealth and poverty (look back to pages 102–4) are the charity putting into practice?
- To complete your study, evaluate the work of Christian Aid. In other words, look at what it is doing and why it is doing it, then make up your own mind about whether you think Christian Aid is successfully putting Christian teachings about wealth and poverty into practice.

ACTIVITIES

2. You might like to reduce your in-depth study of a charity to a grid for ease of reference.
- Column 1: Causes of world poverty (see p. 99)
- Column 2: What the charity is doing in this area?
- Column 3: What link this has with the teachings of Christianity

3. Look at the charity you have studied in detail and note down what it is doing in terms of emergency aid, long-term aid, education and campaigning for a change in attitudes towards world poverty.

4. Look at the countries your charity is targeting and compare them with the map on page 98. What parts of the world are missing out and what parts are getting most of the charity's attention?

6 Islamic teachings about wealth and poverty

AIM

To understand Islamic teachings about wealth and poverty.

STARTER

What do the two cartoons in Figure G tell you about some of the Muslim teachings on wealth and poverty?

The Hadith contains the Prophet Muhammad's teachings. These are some teachings concerning different aspect of wealth and poverty:

A *Richness does not lie in abundance of worldly goods, but true richness is the richness of the soul.*

B *He is not a believer who eats his fill while his neighbour remains hungry by his side.*

C *If you possessed all the gold on the Earth, you could not buy your place in the Hereafter with it.*

D *Riches are sweet, and a source of blessing for him who acquires them by the way; but they are not blessed for him who seeks them out of greed. He is like one who eats but is not filled.*

E *For a person who suffers calamity and loses his property, it is permissible for him to ask until he is able to stand on his own feet.*

The Qur'an says:

F *If your debtor be in straits, grant him a delay until he can discharge his debt; but if you waive the sum as alms it will be better for you, if you but knew it.* (2: 180)

Figure G *These cartoons sum up the Islamic attitude towards the rich exploiting the poor. Write two sentences to explain what is happening in the top cartoon. Write two sentences to explain why Zakah is the complete opposite.*

G *Men are tempted by the lure of women and offspring, of hoarded treasures of gold and silver, of splendid horses, cattle, and plantations. These are the comforts of this life, but far better is the return to God.* (3: 14)

H *Those that give alms by night and by day, in private and in public, shall be rewarded by their Lord. They shall have nothing to fear or to regret.* (2: 274)

I *God has laid His curse on usury (charging interest on money that is lent) and blessed almsgiving with increase.* (2: 276)

J *Let those who hoard the wealth which God has bestowed on them out of His bounty never think it is good for them: it is nothing but evil. The riches they have hoarded shall become their fetters on the Day of Resurrection.* (3: 180)

K *To those that hoard up gold and silver and do not spend it in God's cause, proclaim a woeful punishment.* (9: 34)

PATH TO THE TOP

Learn two scripture quotations that you could use in an exam answer. Make sure you know what each quotation teaches Muslims about wealth and poverty.

ACTIVITY

1. Write down the teachings of Islam about wealth and poverty that are listed below and against each, copy the letter of the scripture quotations that teaches this.

- Muhammad disapproved of begging but he said that people could beg for help if they had lost their home and needed help to get started again.
- It is totally forbidden to charge interest on money that has been loaned to someone.
- Money is not everything, you cannot take it with you when you die.
- Money is given to people by God so they must use it to help others, not keep it doing nothing in the bank.
- A true Muslim would not let a fellow Muslim starve.
- If somebody owes you money and cannot afford to pay, you should let them off.

Muslims take the issue of wealth and poverty seriously. Everyone is equal in the eyes of God who created him or her; it does not matter whether they are rich or poor. This means that Muslims should not look down on the poor nor look up to the rich.

It is the duty of every Muslim to help the members of the ummah who are worse off than themselves.

Wealth is given to people by God so it is no disgrace to be rich. Muslims are taught that money is on loan to people for their lifetime, no one can take it with them when they die. Wealth is a test. God has given money to people and will judge them on the way that they use it. They should not squander money, but use it wisely to help others.

Zakah

It is the duty of every Muslim to give money to charity. Zakah is the third pillar of Islam and all Muslims must give 2.5 per cent of their surplus money to charity. By giving, the remaining money is purified and a Muslim can use it without feeling guilty. Zakah is collected by the mosque. It helps the less fortunate and cleanses the giver's heart of the love of money. Zakah is collected and distributed in private so that no one can feel proud of how much they have given, nor feel ashamed of receiving what is theirs by right.

ACTIVITIES

2. How does giving zakah purify a person's wealth?

3. Look at the meaning of the word '**stewardship**' on page 105. How does that concept fit in with the Muslim teachings on wealth and poverty in quotes A–K?

For discussion

'It is not now much you give that matters, but your attitude when you give.' Would a Muslim agree? Would a charity agree?

FOR RESEARCH

Find out about four charitable causes that Zakah can be used for.

6 Putting Islamic teachings into practice

AIM

To understand how Muslims put Islamic teachings about wealth and poverty into practice.

Sadaqah

In addition to zakah, which Muslims are expected to give because it is one of the five pillars, they are also encouraged to make additional voluntary donations to the needy. **Sadaqah** is any money that is given freely out of compassion for the suffering of another person, no matter whether they are Muslim or not. Coins dropped into a charity collecting tin in the street or a gift to an animal charity would all be forms of sadaqah. Some Muslims leave a bequest to a charity in their will as sadaqah.

*Figure H The charity, Muslim Aid, distributes **qurbani** (meat from an animal sacrifice) to some of the most deprived areas of the world. The charity says: 'A vital part of our humanitarian work is helping our donors to fulfil their religious duties of feeding the fasting in Ramadan and performances of sacrifices in Id-ul-Adha'. When does a Muslim break the fast?*

The Hadith says:

Sadaqah is the responsibility of every Muslim.

His companions said, 'O Prophet of God. What about a person who has nothing to give?'

He said, 'He should work, earn and give in charity.'

They said, 'If he has nothing in spite of this?'

He said, 'He should help a distressed person, one who is in need.'

They said, 'If he is unable to do this?'

He said, 'He should do good deeds and not do bad things, this is charity on his part'.

ACTIVITIES

1. Draw a diagram you could use for revision showing the difference between zakah and sadaqah. (See page 109 for information about zakah). Show how each puts Muslim teachings on wealth and poverty into action.

2. What do you think a Muslim should do if they see a charity collector for the Macmillan Cancer Nursing Care outside a supermarket? Why? Try to use the correct technical term.

Ramadan

The fourth pillar of Islam is **sawm**, fasting during the holy month of **Ramadan**. This makes Muslims more aware of the plight of the poor and needy.

During the hours of daylight, Muslims go without food and drink so they can empathise with the sufferings of the less fortunate. Towards the end of the holy month, extra money is given so the poor can join their fellow Muslims in celebrating the festival of Id. Muslim charities like the one in Figure H, also help distribute this money to the most needy Muslims round the world. In 2004,

Muslim Aid distributed £320,350 to the poor around the world during Ramadan. They also gave out food parcels to widows, orphanages, old people's homes, prisons and hospitals.

ACTIVITY

3. Explain how Ramadan helps Muslims to put Islamic teachings on wealth and poverty into action.

PATH TO THE TOP

Use some appropriate terms to boost your grade. The following are worth learning.

- **compassion** understanding the suffering of people and doing something to help them
- **justice** the idea that everyone has the right to be treated fairly. Everyone has the right to have a decent standard of living because everyone is part of God's creation, all life is sacred and people are equal members of the worldwide family of humanity. It is morally wrong to ignore people's problems, people have a duty to help those worse off than themselves
- **Ramadan** the ninth month when the Qur'an says all Muslims must fast
- **riba** any form of lending or borrowing money at interest which is disapproved of
- **sawm** fasting by going without food and drink during daylight hours (the fourth pillar)
- **stewardship** taking care of something that does not belong to you and using it wisely. Muslims believe that all wealth belongs to God and is given to us to use wisely

Money must be earned honestly

- There is no shame in a Muslim being rich as long as the money has been earned fairly. No one should have been exploited in the process. Zakah purifies the money earned and enables a Muslim to enjoy the fruits of their labour.

- Figure G on page 108 shows that Muslims do not approve of receiving interest on wealth in the bank, because that is making money for the rich at the expense of the poor. There are special Islamic banks where Muslims can keep their money and any profits made are used to help the needy. Islam does not approve of charging interest on loans either, because it is making money out of people who do not have it. Money, therefore, should be loaned without interest and if something unfortunate happens which prevents a person paying the loan off, the debt should be wiped clean.

- The Qur'an forbids gambling because this involves one person gaining money at the expense of a large number of people. Too often gambling becomes obsessive and can lead to suffering.

Figure I *There is no shame in being rich or poor in Islam. It is what you do with your money that matters and Muslims believe God will judge them on this.*

PATH TO THE TOP

Remember that in Islam the poor are *entitled* to receive money from the rich. Muslims believe that is justice. Giving to charity is not a choice, it is an obligation.

RELIGION: WEALTH AND POVERTY

GCSE Religious Studies for Edexcel: Religion and Life with Christianity and Islam (Unit A)   111

6 Muslim Aid

AIM

To understand the link between Islamic teachings and the work of Muslim Aid in their attempts to remove the causes of poverty.

As part of your coursework, or for your final exam, you are required to make a detailed study of the work of one religious agency involved in working for world development and the relief of poverty. If you are studying Islam, you could examine the work of Red Crescent, Islamic Relief or Muslim Aid. We have chosen to focus on Muslim Aid. Access their website by visiting www.heinemann.co.uk/hotlinks, typing in the express code 2299P and clicking on this section. You could choose a different charity if you have access to good material or know a person who works closely with that charity, but make sure that it is a religious one to qualify for this unit of work.

Q For discussion

Muslim Aid uses a quotation from the Qur'an to explain its work. 'Whoever saved a life, it shall be as if he had saved the life of all mankind.' Why is that appropriate to the work of an Islamic charity?

They also say, 'Muslim Aid is providing humanitarian relief and working for poverty eradication'. How does that fit in with the world development solutions referred to on pages 100–1?

The in-depth study

- Find out when the organisation was founded and what happened that started things off. In the case of Muslim Aid, you will be looking at the catastrophes that struck different parts of the world in 1985 and the desire of many Muslims to help relieve suffering.

- Muslim Aid regards itself as a Muslim organisation. Remind yourself of the different aspects of Islamic teachings about wealth and poverty (look back to pages 108–9) and try to see how these are being put into practice. You could look at the case studies on the page opposite or investigate other ways Muslim Aid is helping the ummah.

- Research three different projects that Muslim Aid is currently involved in around the world and write a couple of sentences about each. It would be a good idea to find one project that involves emergency aid, another that is a long-term development and a third that entails educating people.

- To complete your study, evaluate the work of Muslim Aid. In other words, look at what it is doing and why it is doing it, then make up your own mind about whether you think Muslim Aid is successfully putting Islamic teachings about wealth and poverty into practice.

ACTIVITY

1. You might like to reduce your study of a charity to a grid for ease of reference.
- Column 1: Causes of world poverty (see p. 99)
- Column 2: What the charity is doing in this area?
- Column 3: What link this has with the teachings of Islam

CASE STUDY 1: SUPPLYING CLEAN WATER

The charity says:

Muslim Aid's water projects are striving to help poor people to secure access to a clean, safe water supply. By doing this we can reduce health risks and help people affected by drought or unreliable water supplies to support their families better and grow food more effectively.

Why is the provision of clean water particularly important to Muslims? (Hint: think about **wudu**.)

CASE STUDY 2: FIGHTING CHILD BLINDNESS

Muslim Aid says:

1.5 million children in the world suffer from blindness and every year hundreds of thousands of children are born blind or become blind in the course of their early childhood. Medication or surgery can help them regain the gift of sight by the mercy of Allah.

Muslim Aid's preventative and curative programme consists of:

- mobile medical clinics to reach out to the most deprived people
- free eye examinations
- health and hygiene education programmes
- trachoma medication – only £2 can cure a person's blindness
- vitamin A supplementation – only £20 pays for 100 children
- cataract surgery – just £40 can help to restore someone's eyesight.

ACTIVITIES

2. Use the material in the case studies, along with any more information you can get from Muslim Aid's website or from newspaper reports on the Internet to make a leaflet about Muslim Aid's work. Make sure you explain why Muslims should be concerned.

3. Look at the countries your charity is targeting and compare them with the map on page 98. What parts of the world are missing out and what parts are getting most of the charity's attention?

6 Putting it all together

ACTIVITIES

1. Make a list from memory of the causes of poverty in a LEDC.

2. Check your answer against the possible causes listed on page 99. You may have suggested other causes of poverty, which do not appear there, but are equally valid. Check with your teacher.

3. Use your revised list to answer this exam question.

'Outline the causes of world poverty.' **(4)**

To gain a good level, develop the points on your list into at least one sentence each.

Figure J
Poverty often has more than one cause. What might have caused the poverty shown in this photograph?

This section of the exam paper is like the coursework section and usually has three parts to the question.

- The **(a)** part of this question requires a description. In simple terms, the examiner is asking you to say *what* is going on.
- The **(b)** part of the question requires an explanation, so you are being asked to tell the examiner *why* that is happening.
- The **(c)** part of this question is the evaluative part. The exam specification, which appears on page 97, states that you will be asked to make a personal evaluation of the way religion deals with the issue of wealth and poverty. That is what question **(c)** will be about, although you do not know exactly what will be asked. Nevertheless, you can prepare yourself well to answer this sort of question.

Trying out your answers

Working with a partner is a really good way of practising your answers to these questions. You could start with one of you saying, 'Tell me about the work of one of the religious agencies in tackling poverty.' Then reply by giving the name of the religion and the name of one of its charities. Say what sort of things it is doing to help the poor. It would be good if you could name some of the places in the world where it is working.

Tackling an exam question

Here is a **(c)** question from the exam paper.

'You cannot be truly religious and rich.'
Do you agree? Give reasons for your answer showing you have considered another point of view. In your answer you should refer to at least one religion.   **(8)**

Student's answer

I think that you can be religious and rich provided that you spend some of your money helping the poor. ✓ (Level 1) *Being rich is not necessarily a bad thing and it may not be your fault that you are rich. You could have been left a lot of money by a rich uncle or you might have won the jackpot on the lottery. I do not think God would send you to hell for that, after all neither of those things are your fault.*

What is bad about being rich is being greedy and keeping all the money to yourself when there are people starving all round the world. ✓ (Level 2) *It is also bad if money rules your life so that you are always wondering what else you can buy and sell to make more money. You would be a sad person and not have many friends then.*

Examiner's comments

The student starts off by making some good points but he has not read the question carefully. He does mention God, but not the teachings of any particular religion. He has not tackled the issue of whether a rich person can be truly religious either. He has just reached a Level 2. To improve his grade he could explain what his chosen religion teaches about wealth.

Student's improved answer

I think that you can be religious and rich provided that you spend some of your money helping the poor. ✓ (L1) *Being rich is not necessarily a bad thing and it may not be your fault that you are rich. You could have been left a lot of money by a rich uncle or you might have won the jackpot on the lottery. I do not think God would send you to hell for that, after all neither of those things are your fault. What is bad about being rich is being greedy and keeping all the money to yourself when there are people starving all round the world.* ✓ (L2)

Some Christians, however, would agree with the statement because they believe Jesus told his followers to give up all their wealth and follow him. ✓ (L3) *That would mean you couldn't be rich and truly a Christian. However, not all Christians think that. They believe that so long as you give some money to the poor, you can enjoy your wealth. Muslims would agree with that too because they give zakah which is 2.5 per cent of their wealth. That purifies the rest of their money and enables them to do what they like with it.*

In conclusion I think most believers would say you can be truly religious and rich, so long as you are compassionate. ✓ (L4)

Level 1 (2 marks)

For a point of view supported by one relevant reason.

Level 2 (4 marks)

For a basic for and against, or a reasoned opinion, or well argued points of view with no personal opinion.

Level 3 (6 marks)

For a reasoned personal opinion, using religious/moral argument, referring to another point of view.

Level 4 (8 marks)

For a coherent, reasoned personal opinion using religious/moral argument, evaluating another point of view to reach a personal conclusion.

10 a) Try to give 3 or 4 examples and write a sentence explaining why each causes poverty. Page 99 will help you.

b) Begin by saying, 'In Islam ...'. Discuss Muslim teachings and the Muslim view of justice in relation to the poor (see pp. 108–11).

c) This is your chance to give a personal opinion. Say *what* you think then explain *why*. Then say what other people think and explain why they say that. You must make sure that one of those viewpoints is the Christian one and is supported by Christian teachings. These appear on pages 102–5. To gain the highest marks you must come to a personal conclusion, showing you have considered another viewpoint.

The first (c) question is based on a question from the Edexcel Unit A paper 2004. The second (c) question is based on a question from the Edexcel Unit A Specimen Paper.

SECTION FIVE OPTIONS: EXTENDED WRITING

You must answer ONE question from this section. You are advised to spend 30 minutes on this section. You will be assessed on the Quality of Written Communication in this section

EXAMPLE QUESTION 10

10 a) Outline the causes of world poverty. **(4)**

b) Choose **ONE** religion **other than Christianity** and explain why the followers of that religion should try to remove the causes of world poverty. **(8)**

c) *'Christians should give all their wealth to the poor.'*

Do you agree? Give reasons for your opinion, showing you have considered another point of view. **(8)**

(Total 20 marks)

EXAMPLE QUESTION 10

a) Describe the work of one religious agency which helps to relieve poverty. **(4)**

b) Describe how the teachings of that religion may lead the agency to do this work. **(8)**

c) *'You must give a large part of your money away if you want to be religious.'*

Do you agree? Give reasons for your opinion, showing you have considered another point of view. **(8)**

(Total 20 marks)

Leave blank

Q10

Q10

Remember: Although you are being given a choice of two questions on this page, there is no choice in Section Five, Question 10 on the real exam paper.

10 a) State which religious agency you are writing about at the outset. Be sure it is a religious one. Then give 3 or 4 examples of what it is doing to relieve poverty.

b) If the religion is not mentioned in the name of the agency, make sure you state whether it is Christian or Muslim. Give several examples of religious teachings and for each one say what the agency does to put it into practice.

c) Your views are requested so you could begin, 'I think ... because ...'. The best answers will make sure that the views of a Christian or a Muslim are included along with the religious teachings to support that point. Make sure you write about two opposing viewpoints. Make sure you come to a personal conclusion, showing you have considered another viewpoint.

COURSEWORK GUIDANCE

Coursework is an extremely important part of your Religious Studies GCSE. It carries 20 marks of its own, which is the same as one of the other complete units of study on the paper. In addition, 3 marks are awarded for **QWC** which means the **Q**uality of your **W**ritten **C**ommunication – in other words the standard of your English. Added together this now makes that part of your work worth more than any other section of the paper.

What have you got to do?

You are asked to write about 1500 words. That sounds a lot when you first see it written down! Once you start writing, however, you might find it is not enough, but do not be tempted to go over that limit. Equally, do not assume you can get away with writing less! As a rule of thumb try to keep within 10 per cent of the number of words requested. So keep between 1350 and 1650 words.

Starting out – look at the question

This is a Religious Studies exam and the exam board wants you to consider the issue from a religious angle first and foremost. So if you are doing religion and the media coursework, remember to keep in mind that the examiner does not want a media studies answer. The examiner wants to know how religion is portrayed in the media, not who starred in a film or the whole plot.

Equally, when you are looking at wealth and poverty do not get bogged down describing the problems of the poor or offer a geography answer. The examiner is asking you what the members of that religion are doing about the problems.

Begin by analysing the title of the programme/film or the name of the religious organisation. Simply underline or highlight the important words and phrases in it, just as you have learned to do with exam questions.

Part (a)

It is clear that part (a) is the most important because it carries 12 marks. However, part (a) is divided up into three parts, so look at the number of marks the exam board will give you for each bit. Work on part (a) first.

Part (b)

Only when (a) is finished to your satisfaction should you think about tackling part (b). That is because (b) requires a thorough knowledge of the subject before you can give your opinion. This is the evaluative part of the question which you will have been practising on your exam paper work. It is your chance to give your views with the reasons for them and for you to state what those who disagree with you would say along with their reasons.

This part of the paper, the evaluative section, carries 8 marks, which is twice what it was worth on the rest of the paper. Your evaluation of this subject is extremely important.

Question part	Assessment objective criteria	Marks
a) i	Testing assessment objective 1, selecting and deploying knowledge	4 marks
a) ii	Testing assessment objective 2, explaining and understanding religion	4 marks
a) iii	Testing assessment objective 2, explaining and understanding religion	4 marks
b)	Testing assessment objective 3, evaluating different responses to religion and moral issues	8 marks

Research

The Internet is valuable for gaining up-to-date material but use it wisely.

- Not everything that appears there is accurate or useful for your coursework. Useful websites can be accessed by visiting www.heinemann.co.uk/hotlinks and typing in the express code 2299P.
- Always make a note of the name and address of the site you have used so you can put it in your list of sources.
- Do not be tempted to lift whole chunks of material off the Internet. Read and select the best information to use and rewrite it in your own words.

Books are also a useful tool for research. Once again, do not copy large chunks. Read and put in your own words the material you want to include. Keep a note of the title, author, publisher and date of publication to put in your sources. Writing to some of the organisations whose addresses appear on page 136 is also sensible and can often give you a great deal more focused information than the Internet. Do not forget to enclose an SAE if you want a reply.

Writing it up

- When you have assembled the research for the first part of the question, plan the answer.
- Then go ahead and write it up. It can be good to include quotations. Do not use long ones. A couple of sentences at most can be excellent if you go on to say 'that shows…'
- When you read through your work afterwards, check to see if there are any technical terms you could include that might boost your marks.
- When you have finished the final section of the coursework that is the time to read it all through from beginning to end. It is surprising how much easier it is to polish it up when you have had a few days break from the text.
- Polishing up not only invloves re-reading and amending the material, it also includes the QWC; those vital 3 marks that are awarded for legible handwriting, generally accurate spelling, punctuation and grammar. Check that you have written in sentences (no bullet points here or you will be throwing marks away) and that you have used paragraphs. Add a list of the material you used in your research.

These are the levels the examiner will use to mark part **(a)**.
- **Level 1 (1–3 marks)** For isolated examples of simple, relevant knowledge or understanding.
- **Level 2 (4–6 marks)** For basic knowledge or understanding of a relevant idea presented in a structured way.
- **Level 3 (7–9 marks)** For a developed description/explanation showing an understanding of the main idea(s) and deploying a limited range of specialist vocabulary.
- **Level 4 (10–12 marks)** For a coherent and comprehensive description/explanation showing a full understanding of the main idea(s) using specialist terms appropriately and with precision.

These are the levels the examiner will use to mark part **(b)**.
- **Level 1 (1–2 marks)** For an opinion supported by one relevant reason.
- **Level 2 (3–4 marks)** For a basic 'for and against', or a reasoned opinion supported by religious/moral evidence or examples, presented in a structured form.
- **Level 3 (5–6 marks)** For a structured and reasoned evaluation, using religious/moral argument, evidence or examples, referring to another point of view and deploying a limited range of specialist vocabulary.
- **Level 4 (7–8 marks)** For a coherent and reasoned evaluation, based on religious/moral argument, evidence or examples, giving an account of an alternative point of view to reach a personal conclusion using specialist terms appropriately and with precision.

Your personal exam number goes in here. Take care writing it down because the number is important to the exam board when recording your score.

Here you fill in the school's exam number.

You print your surname here and your initials go afterwards. Your signature goes in the box below. These are all additional safeguards to ensure that the exam board has awarded the marks for this exam paper to the right candidate.

These columns are for each question on the paper. When you have finished answering your paper, go back to the front and circle the numbers of the questions you have chosen to answer. Leave the right-hand column of boxes blank because the examiner will put the marks you have scored in it.

These two boxes are left blank by you. The examiner will enter the total marks for the paper in the top box. When the examiner's marking is checked by the leader of the examining team, the team leader puts his or her total mark in the lower box. They should be the same. If for any reason the marks are very different, the paper will be marked again. That way you know that you are getting a fair, correct mark for your work.

In this box the examiner will write the total you have scored on the questions in the exam paper.

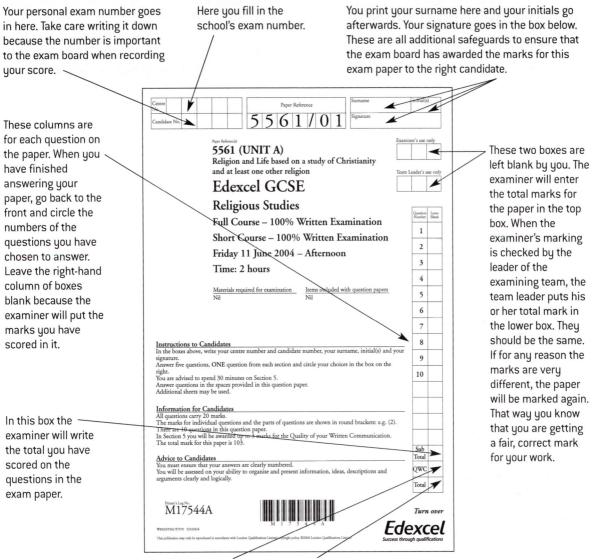

In this box the examiner will write the mark for your **QWC** (**Q**uality of **W**ritten **C**ommunication). This is the mark out of three which you have been awarded for your use of English in the extended writing question. If you did coursework, those marks will have been awarded there and will not appear on the exam paper.

In this final box the examiner will write your total mark for this paper, adding in the QWC if necessary. The total for candidates who did the extended writing question will be out of 103 and the paper will be out of 80 for candidates who did coursework. This is because the coursework is marked out of 23.

The diagram above shows the front cover of the GCSE exam paper. This paper has ten questions on it because it contains questions 9 and 10 for the extended writing tasks. If you have chosen to do coursework for your exam, then the front cover you will see will only have questions 1 to 8.

These instructions, information and advice will always appear on the front of the paper. It is worth reading it carefully now. Check you understand it. Now is a good opportunity to ask your teacher about anything you are not sure of here.

Exam focus on the (a) questions

Answering the (a) questions

The **(a)** questions are short questions to start you off on each page of the exam paper. You just have to give the meaning of a word. There are a set number of key terms in each unit of study and the exam paper can only ask you the meaning of one of those words. With careful preparation you can guarantee that you pick up those 2 marks every time.

HINT

The exam paper is only asking for a definition, that is the meaning of this important word. You only have to write one sentence so do not be tempted to go on for a paragraph. You need to write down the essence of that word or expression in your definition. Look at the definitions given in the glossary; they are good to learn and fix in your mind.

Key terms

The full list of key terms for each unit appears on the opening page of the unit. Meanings are also given during the course of the unit and all the key terms are defined in the glossary on pages 138–40.

- With a partner you could test each other on the meanings.
- On your own you can test yourself by copying down each word. Next write down what you think the meaning is. Then check it against the glossary.
- Another way of learning the key terms is to write the word on one scrap of paper and the meaning on another. When you have got a little pile of key terms and their meanings, try matching the correct pairs.

The key terms for Section 1, Believing in God, are:

numinous, conversion, miracle, prayer, design argument, causation argument, agnosticism, atheism, moral evil, natural evil, omnipotent, benevolent, omniscient

The key terms for Section 2, Matters of life and death, are:

resurrection, immortality of the soul, paranormal, abortion, sanctity of life, euthanasia, assisted suicide, voluntary euthanasia, non-voluntary euthanasia

The key terms for Section 3, Marriage and the family, are:

cohabitation, marriage, faithfulness, pre-marital sex, promiscuity, adultery, re-marriage, nuclear family, extended family, re-constituted family

The key terms for Section 4, Social harmony, are:

equality, sexism, multi-ethnic society, prejudice, discrimination, racism, racial harmony, multi-faith society, religious freedom, religious pluralism

Please note:

The information given about (a), (b), (c) and (d) questions on pages 120–3 relates to questions in Sections 1–4 of the exam paper. The questions in Section 5, the extend writing option, have different requirements. See pages 94–6, 114–16 and 132–5 for guidance on how to answer Section 5 questions.

Exam focus on the (b) questions

Answering the (b) questions

There are three types of (b) questions.

1. Some (b) questions might ask you to 'outline' something. The examiner is expecting more than one point or reason to be given. It is expected that each reason will take you up to another level. In some cases, two reasons could take you up to Level 3, but three reasons would stay at Level 2 if they were limited in structure.

   With an 'outline' question, at least two or more reasons are necessary to reach Level 3. If you just list your reasons, you will not reach more than Level 2. A list counts as a limited structure. The examiner wants you to discuss each point you have given.

   To plan your answer to an 'outline' question it might be a good idea to list three or four bullet points in the margin in rough. Arrange them in the most logical order so that one can lead on to the next. Then write a sentence about each to form an answer.

2. Other (b) questions could ask you to **describe** something. Once again the examiner is looking for a concise and organised account. As part of your planning, jot down three or four points in the margin that you want to include in your answer. Arrange them in the most logical order. See if there are any specialist terms you can use.

3. Some (b) questions begin by asking you to choose **ONE** religion **other than Christianity**. That means you will write about Islam. Always begin your answer, 'In Islam…' so the examiner is in no doubt what religion you have chosen to write about.

Example questions

Here are some examples of (b) questions from different areas of study in this book. Read them through to familiarise yourself with this type of question.

- Outline the arguments against belief in life after death. **(6)**
- Outline the views of **ONE** religion **other than Christianity** on the roles of men and women. **(6)**
- Choose **ONE** religion **other than Christianity** and outline the teachings of that religion which help to promote racial harmony. **(6)**
- Outline the reasons a person might give for being an atheist. **(6)**
- Choose **ONE** religion and describe the main features of a religious upbringing in that religion. **(6)**

Choose one of the questions to practise a (b) answer.

These are the levels the examiner will use to mark the (b) questions in Sections 1–4 of the exam paper.

- **Level 1 (2 marks)** For an isolated example of relevant knowledge.
- **Level 2 (4 marks)** For basic relevant knowledge presented within a limited structure.
- **Level 3 (6 marks)** For an organised outline/description, using relevant knowledge with limited use of specialist vocabulary.

Answering the (c) questions

The **(c)** questions on the exam paper carry more marks than any of the other parts on the paper. They are worth 8 marks.

The **(c)** questions often begin with the words 'Explain how…' or 'Explain why…' The examiner is trying to discover two things in these questions:

- do you know **what** a believer does or thinks
- do you understand **why** they do or think that?

It is a **what** and **why** question. You are looking at a belief that makes people behave in a certain way. The more detail you can give in this answer the better the level you will attain. With 8 marks at stake the examiner is looking for some detail.

Different attitudes

Some **(c)** questions ask you to write about the different attitudes that exist within the same religion about a particular issue. These can be nice questions to answer because they fall neatly into three parts.

1. What are the different attitudes believers have about this subject? This will be a brief opening sentence or two which sums up the basic differences within the religion.
2. Why does each group think that? This is the main point of your answer and will explain in detail what each group thinks, and the religious reasons they would give for their views.
3. Conclude with a short sentence explaining why there is variation within the religion. Often the different views hinge on the interpretation of passages in Holy books.

Key terms

Do not forget that the highest levels in this question, as in all of the questions, will go to candidates who can use specialist terms correctly. Think back to the key terms you learned when you studied that unit and see if there is opportunity to use one of these terms in your answer to demonstrate to the examiner that you have a good understanding of the subject.

Example questions

The **(c)** questions give you a chance to show the examiner you understand the issues you have studied. Here are some examples of **(c)** questions from different areas of study in this book. Read them through to familiarise yourself with this type of question.

- Explain why there are different attitudes to life after death among Christians. **(8)**
- Explain how the Muslim community supports family life. **(8)**
- Explain why there are different attitudes to re-marriage in Christianity. **(8)**
- Explain why there are different attitudes to abortion among Muslims. **(8)**
- Explain why there are different views amongst Christians about the role of women in church. **(8)**

Choose one of these questions to practise a **(c)** answer.

These are the levels the examiner will use to mark the **(c)** questions in Sections 1–4 of the exam paper.

- **Level 1 (2 marks)** For a simple, appropriate and relevant idea.
- **Level 2 (4 marks)** For a basic explanation showing understanding of a relevant idea.
- **Level 3 (6 marks)** For a developed explanation showing understanding of the main idea(s), using some specialist vocabulary.
- **Level 4 (8 marks)** For a comprehensive explanation showing a coherent understanding of the main idea(s) and using specialist language appropriately.

Answering the (d) questions

The **(d)** questions on the exam paper are the ones that ask you to express your opinion. You are free to agree or disagree. That will not affect your marks. What makes a difference to your marks is how well you back up your case.

The **(d)** questions are evaluative. It is the only time the examiner asks you what you actually think about an issue. You also have to show that you know about, and can state, the opposite side of the argument – what somebody who does not agree with you would say, and why they would say that. Finally, sum up by saying whether you agree or disagree with the statement and briefly restate your reason in light of the arguments for and against.

Don't forget, your answer must include details of what a Christian or a Muslim would think.

HINTS

When you have finished your answer to one of the example questions, use the examiner's grid to see which level you have achieved. Put a tick on the spot where you think you have earned the mark each time.

Look at your bullet points. What level do you think you would have achieved? Look back at the relevant pages in this book and see if there are any further bullet points you could add to your plan to bring your answer up to a level 4 (4 marks). Arrange your plan into at least three paragraphs then write your answer up in full.

Remember, the (d) question always begins with a quotation. It will give one side of an argument. The examiner wants you to show that you can see where that person is coming from and can understand why they say that.

Example questions

Here are some examples of **(d)** questions from different areas of study in this book. Read them through to familiarise yourself with this type of question.

- *'God and evil can't both exist.'* Do you agree? Give reasons for your opinion, showing you have considered another point of view. **(4)**
- *'If marriage vows are going to be meaningful, then people shouldn't be able to break them whenever they feel like it.'* Do you agree? Give reasons for your answer showing that you have thought about another point of view. **(4)**
- *'Near death experiences prove there is life after death.'* Do you agree? Give reasons for your opinion, showing that you have considered another point of view. **(4)**
- *'Religion is the mainstay of a family.'* Do you agree? Give reasons for your answer showing that you have considered another point of view. **(4)**
- *'Abortion is never an act of love.'* Do you agree? Give reasons for your opinion, showing that you have considered another point of view. In your answer you should refer to Christianity. **(4)**

Choose one of these questions to practise a **(d)** answer.

These are the levels the examiner will use to mark the **(d)** questions in Sections 1–4 of the exam paper.

- **Level 1 (1 mark)** For a point of view supported by one relevant reason.
- **Level 2 (2 marks)** For a basic for and against, or a reasoned opinion, or well argued points of view with no personal opinion.
- **Level 3 (3 marks)** For a reasoned personal opinion, using religious/moral argument, referring to another point of view.
- **Level 4 (4 marks)** For a coherent, reasoned personal opinion, using religious/moral argument, evaluating another point of view to reach a personal conclusion.

	Leave blank
SECTION ONE: BELIEVING IN GOD You must answer ONE question from this section. **EITHER QUESTION 1** **1. a)** What does *prayer* mean? **(2)** **b)** State, with examples, what is meant by moral evil. **(6)** **c)** Choose **ONE** religion and explain how being brought up as a follower of that religion could support a person's belief in God. **(8)** **d)** *'God must exist because so many people believe in him.'* Do you agree? Give reasons for your opinion, showing you have considered another point of view. **(4)** **(Total 20 marks)**	**Q1**
OR QUESTION 2 **2. a)** What is meant by *natural evil*? **(2)** **b)** Describe **ONE** miracle. **(6)** **c)** Explain how the appearance of design in the world may lead to or support belief in God. **(8)** **d)** *'Giving children a religious upbringing is the best start in life they could have.'* Do you agree? Give reasons for your answer showing you have considered another point of view. **(4)** **(Total 20 marks)**	**Q2**

Questions 1(a), 1(d), 2 (b) and 2 (c) have all been taken from the Edexcel Unit A paper 2003.

Questions (a) and (c) are taken from and question (b) is based on a question from the Edexcel Unit A paper 2003.

	Leave blank
EXTRA PRACTICE QUESTION	
a) Name **TWO** types of religious experience. **(2)**	
b) Outline the main features of a religious upbringing in **ONE** religion. **(6)**	
c) Explain why the existence of evil and suffering may cause problems for people who believe in God. **(8)**	
d) *'Unanswered prayers prove there is no God.'* Do you agree? Give reasons for your opinion, showing you have considered another point of view. **(4)**	
(Total 20 marks)	

Remember:
There will only be a choice of two not three questions in Section One on the real exam paper.

Worked example for you to mark

2 b) Describe **ONE** miracle. **(6)**

A miracle is an event which seems to defy natural laws. Religious believers would say the event happened because God intervened in human life.

One example of a miracle might involve a Christian who was suffering from an illness that the doctors said was incurable. The person would probably pray to God to help them get better and if they were Roman Catholic they might go on a pilgrimage to Lourdes. Lourdes is a holy site where healing miracles have taken place. If the Christian got better from their illness they would think their prayers had been answered and a miracle had taken place.

What level do you think this answer would achieve?

- **Level 1 (2 marks)** For an isolated example of relevant knowledge.
- **Level 2 (4 marks)** For basic relevant knowledge presented within a limited structure.
- **Level 3 (6 marks)** For an organised outline/description, using relevant knowledge with limited use of specialist vocabulary.

Exam focus on matters of life and death

	Leave blank

SECTION TWO: MATTERS OF LIFE AND DEATH

You must answer ONE question from this section.

EITHER QUESTION 3

3. **a)** What does *resurrection* mean? **(2)**
   b) Outline the British law on abortion. **(6)**
   c) Choose **ONE** religion **other than Christianity** and explain why the followers of that religion believe in life after death. **(8)**
   d) *'People who are suffering should be allowed to take their own life.'*
   Do you agree? Give reasons for your opinion, showing you have considered another point of view. In your answer you should refer to at least one religion. **(4)** **Q3**

   (Total 20 marks)

OR QUESTION 4

4. **a)** What does *immortality* mean? **(2)**
   b) Outline Christian teachings about life after death. **(6)**
   c) Explain the different attitudes towards euthanasia in **ONE** religion **other than Christianity**. **(8)**
   d) *'All good people go to heaven no matter what they believe.'*
   Do you agree? Give reasons for your opinion, showing that you have considered another point of view. In your answer, you should refer to at least one religion. **(4)** **Q4**

   (Total 20 marks)

Question 3(a) is taken from the Edexcel Unit A paper 2004. Questions 3(c), 3(d) and 4(a) are based on questions from the Edexcel Unit A Specimen Paper. Question 4(d) is based on a question from Edexcel Unit A paper 2003.

<table>
<tr><td>

EXTRA PRACTICE QUESTION

a) Give **TWO** examples of the paranormal.
(2)

b) Outline the teachings of **ONE** religion **other than Christianity** on euthanasia.
(6)

c) Explain why some people do not believe in life after death.
(8)

d) *'Life is sacred and should be preserved at all costs.'*
Do you agree? Give reasons for your opinion, showing you have considered another point of view. In your answer you should refer to at least one religion.
(4)

(Total 20 marks)

</td><td>

Leave blank

</td></tr>
</table>

Remember:
There will only be a choice of two not three questions in Section Two on the real exam paper.

Questions (a) and (c) are taken from the Edexcel Unit A paper 2003. Question (b) is based on a question from the Edexcel Unit A paper 2004.

Worked example for you to mark

c) Explain why some people do not believe in life after death. **(8)**

Some people say that life after death cannot possibly exist because there is no evidence. Nobody who has died has ever come back to tell us about it. When the body dies, everything dies. That has been shown to be the case when people have to make difficult decisions to do with switching off a life-support machine. In cases like this, the brain always dies before the body, so that means there cannot be anything left to go on for eternity.

Also people who do not believe in life after death say that death means the end of life. It does not make sense to talk about life after death; that is illogical.

What level do you think this answer would achieve?
- **Level 1 (2 marks)** For a simple, appropriate and relevant idea.
- **Level 2 (4 marks)** For a basic explanation showing understanding of a relevant idea.
- **Level 3 (6 marks)** For a developed explanation showing understanding of the main idea(s), using some specialist vocabulary.
- **Level 4 (8 marks)** For a comprehensive explanation showing a coherent understanding of the main idea(s) and using specialist language appropriately.

	Leave blank
SECTION THREE: MARRIAGE AND THE FAMILY You must answer ONE question from this section. **EITHER QUESTION 5** **5. a)** What is *adultery*? **(2)** **b)** Outline the teachings of **ONE** religion **other than Christianity** about family life. **(6)** **c)** Explain why there are different attitudes towards divorce and re-marriage in Christianity. **(8)** **d)** *'A religious wedding ceremony helps to make a marriage work.'* Do you agree? Give reasons for your opinion, showing you have considered another point of view. In your answer you should refer to at least one religion. **(4)** **(Total 20 marks)**	Q5
OR QUESTION 6 **6. a)** What is a *re-marriage?* **(2)** **b)** Choose **ONE** religion **other than Christianity** and outline the marriage ceremony. **(6)** **c)** Explain why family life is important to Christians. **(8)** **d)** *'Marriage is the only place for sex.'* Do you agree? Give reasons for your opinion, showing you have considered another point of view. In your answer you should refer to at least one religion. **(4)** **(Total 20 marks)**	Q6

Question 5(b) and (c) are based on questions from the Edexcel Unit A paper 2004. Question 5(d) is taken from the Edexcel Unit A paper 2003.

Remember:
There will only be a choice of two not three questions in Section Three on the real exam paper.

EXTRA PRACTICE QUESTION

Leave blank

a) What is a *nuclear family*? **(2)**

b) Outline the different Christian attitudes towards divorce. **(6)**

c) Explain how a religious wedding ceremony in **ONE** religion can help a marriage to succeed. **(8)**

d) *'Children do not need a mother and father who are married to each other.'* Do you agree? Give reasons for your opinion, showing you have considered another point of view. In your answer you should refer to at least one religion. **(4)**

(Total 20 marks)

Question (b) is based on a question from and question (d) is taken from the Edexcel Unit A paper 2004.

Worked example for you to mark

6 d) *'Marriage is the only place for sex.'*

Do you agree? Give reasons for your opinion, showing you have considered another point of view. In your answer you should refer to at least one religion. **(4)**

Some people say that you should not have pre-marital sex because it is wrong. Muslims would agree with this because the Qur'an teaches that all forms of sex outside marriage are adultery and this carries harsh punishments.

People who disagree that you have to be married to have sex would say that sex is acceptable in a loving relationship. Some liberal Christians accept pre-marital sex between a couple who are committed to each other and plan to marry. Some people believe it is better for a couple to live together in a sexual relationship before they marry than to find out later that they are incompatible and have to get divorced.

Overall, I think sex is acceptable before marriage because it is an act of love, but I do not agree with extra-marital sex because people can get hurt.

What level do you think this answer would achieve?

- **Level 1 (1 mark)** For a point of view supported by one relevant reason.
- **Level 2 (2 marks)** For a basic for and against, or a reasoned opinion, or well argued points of view with no personal opinion.
- **Level 3 (3 marks)** For a reasoned personal opinion, using religious/moral argument, referring to another point of view.
- **Level 4 (4 marks)** For a coherent, reasoned personal opinion, using religious/moral argument, evaluating another point of view to reach a personal conclusion.

	Leave blank
SECTION FOUR: SOCIAL HARMONY	

You must answer ONE question from this section.

EITHER QUESTION 7

7. **a)** What is *religious freedom*? **(2)**
   b) Outline the teachings of **ONE** religion **other than Christianity** towards racial harmony. **(6)**
   c) Explain the different attitudes towards the roles of men and women in Christianity. **(8)**
   d) *'Living in a multi-faith society is difficult for a believer.'*
   Do you agree? Give reasons for your opinion, showing you have considered another point of view. In your answer you should refer to at least one religion. **(4)** **Q7**

(Total 20 marks)

OR QUESTION 8

8. **a)** Give an example of *sexism*. **(2)**
   b) Outline the teachings of Christianity regarding the roles of men and women. **(6)**
   c) Explain why prejudice and discrimination cause problems in a multi-ethnic society. **(8)**
   d) *'Trying to convert people to your religion is wrong.'*
   Do you agree? Give reasons for your opinion, showing you have considered another point of view. In your answer you should refer to at least one religion. **(4)** **Q8**

(Total 20 marks)

Questions 7(a) and 8(c) are taken from the Edexcel Unit A paper 2004.
Questions 7(b) and (c) are based on questions from the Edexcel Unit A paper 2004.

	Leave blank

EXTRA PRACTICE QUESTION

a) Name **TWO** religions **other than Christianity** practised in the UK. **(2)**

b) Choose **ONE** religion **other than Christianity** and outline its attitudes to other religions. **(6)**

c) Explain how the teachings of Christianity may help racial harmony. **(8)**

d) *'Men and women are different so you can't expect to have equality.'*
Do you agree? Give reasons for your opinion, showing you have considered another point of view. In your answer you should refer to at least one religion. **(4)**

(Total 20 marks)

Question (a) is taken from the Edexcel Unit A Specimen paper. Question (b) is taken from the Edexcel Unit A paper 2004. Question (c) is based on a question from the Edexcel Unit A paper 2003.

Remember: There will only be a choice of two not three questions in Section Four on the real exam paper.

Worked example for you to mark

8 b) Outline the teachings of Christianity regarding the roles of men and women. **(6)**

Christianity teaches that men and women were created equal in the sight of God. Some evangelical Christians teach that although men and women are equal they have different roles to fulfil in the home and in the church. They support this with the teachings of St Paul in the Bible.

More liberal Christians teach that because men and women were created equal, they have equal roles in the church and in the home. These Christians look at Jesus' treatment of women in the Bible and consider that St Paul taught that men and women are equal in the sight of Christ.

Roman Catholic Christians accept men and women as having equal roles but teach that only men can become priests because Jesus chose men as his apostles.

What level do you think this answer would achieve?
- **Level 1 (2 marks)** For an isolated example of relevant knowledge.
- **Level 2 (4 marks)** For basic relevant knowledge presented within a limited structure.
- **Level 3 (6 marks)** For an organised outline/description, deploying relevant knowledge with limited use of specialist vocabulary.

	Leave blank

SECTION FIVE OPTIONS: EXTENDED WRITING

You must answer ONE question from this section. You are advised to spend 30 minutes on this section. You will be assessed on the Quality of Written Communication in this section.

EXAMPLE QUESTION 9

a) Outline the variety and range of specifically religious programmes on television. **(4)**

b) Choose an important religious or moral theme and explain how it was dealt with by a soap opera, or in the press. **(8)**

c) *'The media never treats religion fairly.'* Do you agree? Give reasons for your opinion, showing you have considered another point of view. **(8)**

Q9

(Total 20 marks)

EXAMPLE QUESTION 9

a) Describe the way a religious or moral theme was handled in a soap opera or by the national press. **(4)**

b) Explain why some people might find a religious broadcast interesting. **(8)**

c) *'Religious documentaries are boring.'* Do you agree? Give reasons for your opinion, showing you have considered another point of view. **(8)**

Q9

(Total 20 marks)

Remember:
Although you are being given a choice of three questions on these pages, there is no choice in Section Five, Question 9 on the real exam paper.

The first (a) question is taken from the Edexcel Unit A paper 2003. The first (c) question is based on a question from the Edexcel Unit A Specimen Paper.

<table>
<tr><td colspan="2">

EXAMPLE QUESTION 9

a) Outline the content of one specifically religious broadcast on television. **(4)**

b) Choose a religious theme from a film or television drama (**not** a soap opera) and explain how the theme was dealt with. **(8)**

c) *'Soap operas are a good way of dealing with a sensitive topic.'* **or** *'The national press are good at dealing with a sensitive topic.'*

Do you agree? Give reasons for your opinion, showing you have considered another point of view. **(8)**

</td><td>Leave blank

Q9</td></tr>
</table>

(Total 20 marks)

Question (b) is taken from the Edexcel Unit A paper 2003. Question (c) is based on a question from the Edexcel Unit A paper 2004.

Worked example for you to mark

9 a) Outline the variety and range of specifically religious programmes on television. **(4)**

There are a wide variety of religious programmes on television but the majority are Christian. There are those which are worship-type programmes. These take the form of an act of worship which the viewers at home can take part in. To help them take part, the programme often puts the words of hymns on the screen so the viewer can sing along. Songs of Praise is a good example of this. At Christmas there are services of carols and Bible readings.

There are also magazine-type programmes that are specifically religious. In this sort of programme the presenter might interview a person about their religious beliefs or discuss an issue with a panel or show a film clip about a relevant religious subject. The Heaven and Earth Show is a popular magazine-type programme. There are also religious documentaries on television sometimes. I watched an interesting one about Muslims going on Hajj. People talked about their thoughts beforehand and at different times on the pilgrimage.

What level do you think this answer would achieve?

- **Level 1 (1 mark)** For an isolated example of relevant knowledge.
- **Level 2 (2 marks)** For basic relevant knowledge presented within a limited structure.
- **Level 3 (3 marks)** For an organised outline/description, using relevant knowledge with limited use of specialist vocabulary.
- **Level 4 (4 marks)** For a comprehensive outline/description using specialist vocabulary appropriately within a coherent structure.

Exam focus on religion: wealth and poverty

SECTION FIVE OPTIONS – EXTENDED WRITING

You must answer ONE question from this section. You are advised to spend 30 minutes on this section. You will be assessed on the Quality of Written Communication in this section.

EXAMPLE QUESTION 10

a) Outline the common causes of poverty in less developed countries. **(4)**

b) Choose **ONE** religion **other than Christianity** and explain how its followers could help to remove the causes of world poverty. **(8)**

c) *'True Christians aren't rich.'*
Do you agree? Give reasons for your opinion, showing you have considered another point of view. **(8)**

(Total 20 marks)

Q10

EXAMPLE QUESTION 10

a) Outline the way one religious agency is working to relieve world poverty. **(4)**

b) Explain how that agency's work is based on the teachings of the religion. **(8)**

c) *'Charity is the only way to solve world poverty.'*
Do you agree? Give reasons for your opinion, showing you have considered another point of view. **(8)**

(Total 20 marks)

Q10

Leave blank

Remember:
Although you are being given a choice of three questions on these pages, there is no choice in Section Five, Question 10 on the real exam paper.

The first (b) question is based on a question from the Edexcel Unit A paper 2004.

EXAMPLE QUESTION 10

a) Outline the teachings of **ONE** religion **other than Christianity** on wealth. **(4)**

b) Explain why Christians should assist in removing the causes of world poverty. **(8)**

c) *'World poverty is caused by selfishness.'* Do you agree? Give reasons for your opinion, showing you have considered another point of view. **(8)**

(Total 20 marks)

Leave blank

Q10

Worked example for you to mark

b) Explain how that agency's work is based on the teachings of the religion. **(8)**

The work of Muslim Aid is based on the teachings of the Qur'an and the Hadith. One of the five pillars of Islam is zakah, which requires Muslims to give 2.5 per cent of their wealth to charity. This purifies the remaining money and helps the needy.

Muslim Aid is one of the charities that assists in the distribution of that money in the correct way. This helps both the giver and the recipient. Muslim Aid also helps Muslims fulfil their duties at Ramadan. By collecting the extra money that has been given in the holy month, Muslim Aid is able to distribute it to those in need so they can enjoy Id. Qurbani, meat which has been sacrificed, is also distributed to the needy by Muslim Aid.

Muslims also give sadaqah, and donations like this can be used by Muslim Aid to assist anyone who is in need, no matter what religion they are. Muslim Aid promotes the ummah by collecting money from Muslims to help other needy Muslims in Britain and around the world.

What level do you think this answer would achieve?
- **Level 1 (2 marks)** For a simple, appropriate and relevant idea.
- **Level 2 (4 marks)** For a basic explanation showing understanding of a relevant idea.
- **Level 3 (6 marks)** For a developed explanation showing understanding of the main idea(s), using some specialist vocabulary.
- **Level 4 (8 marks)** For a comprehensive explanation showing a coherent understanding of the main idea(s) and using specialist language appropriately.

USEFUL ADDRESSES

Action Around Bethlehem Children with Disability
16A Park View Road,
London N3 2JB

CAFOD
Romero Close,
London SW9 9TY

Children's Society
Edward Rudolf House,
Margery Street,
London WC1 0JL

Christian Aid
35 Lower Marsh,
London SE1 7RL

Church of England
London Diocesan House,
36 Causton Street,
London SW1P 4AU

Equal Opportunities Commission
Arndale House,
Arndale Centre,
Manchester M4 3EQ

Help the Hospices
Hospice House,
34–44 Britannia Street,
London WC1 9JB

Islamic Aid
47 Theydon Street,
London E17 8N

Islamic Relief
19 Rea Street South,
Birmingham B5 6LB

Methodist Homes for the Aged
South and East Office,
Barrat House,
668 Hitchin Road,
Stopsley,
Luton LU2 7XH

Muslim Aid
PO Box 3,
London E1 1WP

Muslim Care
206–208 Brick Lane,
London E1 6SA

Muslim Hands – United for the Needy
205 Radford Road,
Hyson Green,
Nottingham NG7 5GT

NSPCC
Weston House,
42 Curtain Road,
London EC2A 3NH

OXFAM
Oxfam House,
274 Banbury Road,
Oxford OX2 7FY

Red Crescent
International Federation of Red Cross and Red Crescent Societies,
PO Box 372,
CH-1211 Geneva,
Switzerland

Silver Ring Thing
530 Moon Clinton Road,
Moon Twp,
PA 15108

Tearfund
100 Church Road,
Teddington,
Middlesex TW11 8QE

The Catholic Truth Society
38/40 Eccleston Square,
London SW1V 1PD

The Salvation Army
101 Newington Causeway,
London SE1 6BN

To access the websites for these organisations please visit www.heinemann.co.uk/hotlinks and click on the useful addresses section. If you wish to email these organisations rather than sending a letter, their email addresses can be found on their websites.

Throughout this book, opportunities are included for pupils to engage with key skills as recommended in the specification, particularly in communication, working with others and ICT.

Communication

Pupils are given the chance to hold discussions. Discussion activities are flagged up throughout the book by the following icon: ⬭. These discussions can take place in pairs, small groups or as whole class debates. For example:

- page 33 – a class debate on whether or not euthanasia should be legalized in the UK.
- page 79 – paired discussion on how religion might be involved with propaganda.

Group discussions can be managed in different ways, for example, pupils could start off in pairs, then regroup into fours. Alternatively, pupils can work in fours or fives, then nominate a spokesperson to feed back to the whole class.

Many of the tasks require pupils to read and summarise information, record information and write in a variety of ways and make presentations. For example:

- activity 1, page 99 – pupils interpret information about poverty from a map, and then use that information to write a press release on behalf of a charity campaigning against poverty.
- activity 1, page 107 – pupils use information in case studies and on the Internet to make a leaflet about Christian Aid's work in Darfur.

Methods of recording and presenting information can also incorporate elements of the information technology key skill.

Information technology

Pupils are given opportunities to use ICT for research and presentation throughout this GCSE course.

Research activities are highlighted when they occur and are always focused. Pupils are provided with websites to use as a starting point for this. For example:

- activity 3, page 20 – pupils are required to find out more about the different religious experiences that people might have had at Lourdes. They are then asked to relate what they find out to how these experiences might affect someone's belief in God.
- for research box, page 49 – pupils are required to find out how the Methodist Church cares for the elderly in the UK.

Pupils can also use ICT to present their work in a variety of ways. For example:

- activity 1, page 25 – pupils can put together a PowerPoint presentation showing the contrasting view people hold about life after death.
- activity 4, page 74 – pupils can create a poster to show the different views Christians hold about the roles of men and women within the church.

Working with others

Many of the tasks encourage pupils to work collaboratively in both one to one and group situations to produce an outcome. For example:

- activity 1, page 26 – pupils work in groups of four to analyse a passage from the Bible.
- activity 4, page 31 – pupils are required to engage in a role play between a pregnant girl and her boyfriend.

GLOSSARY

abortion the removal of a foetus from the womb before it can survive

adultery an act of sexual intercourse between a married person and someone other than their marriage partner

agnosticism not being sure whether God exists

akhirah the Islamic belief in everlasting life after death – the hereafter

almsgiving an old-fashioned word that means giving to charity

assisted suicide providing a seriously ill person with the means to commit suicide

atheism believing that God does not exist

barzakh the period of waiting between death and judgement in Islam

believer a person who is convinced of the truth of a religion

benevolent the belief that God is good/kind

causation argument the idea that everything has been caused (started off) by something else

celibate a person who chooses not to marry or have sex

circumcision the surgical removal of the foreskin of the penis for religious reasons in Islam

cohabitation living together without being married

communion of saints the bond between all Christians alive and dead, living on earth or in heaven

compassion understanding the suffering of people and doing something to help them

conversion when your life is changed by giving yourself to God

Creed a statement of Christian beliefs

design argument when things are connected and seem to have a purpose, e.g. the eye is designed for seeing

developed countries countries where most people have a good standard of living and a high life expectancy

developing countries countries moving towards a more prosperous standard of living

discrimination putting prejudice into practice and treating people less favourably because of their race/gender/colour/class

doctrine of double effect the idea that deciding to perform one action can trigger another. For example, a woman might receive treatment for cancer of the womb that, in the process, kills her unborn child. This would not be classed as abortion because the doctor set out to cure the cancer, not to cause an abortion

ensoulment the moment at 120 days when God gives a foetus a soul (in Islam)

equality the state of everyone having equal rights regardless of gender/race/class

euthanasia an easy and gentle death

exclusivism only selected groups can take part

extended family children, parents and grandparents/aunts/uncles living as a unit or in close proximity

faithfulness staying with your marriage partner and having sex only with them

global village in the 21st century transport and communication links are so swift that we can contact people anywhere on the planet as easily as we can contact people in a neighbouring village

Hadith the sayings of the Prophet Muhammad, as recounted by his household, progeny and companions. These are a major source of Islamic law

Hajj the fifth pillar of Islam which says that every Muslim who is fit enough and can afford it should go on pilgrimage to Makkah once in their lifetime

halal any action or thing which is permitted or lawful for a Muslim

ihram the white clothes worn by male pilgrims on Hajj. They are made of simple pieces of white seamless cotton and show everyone is equal in the sight of God

immortality of the soul the idea that the soul lives on after the death of the body

inclusivism everyone can take part

jahannam the Islamic name for hell, which means 'the place of fire'

jannah the Islamic name for heaven, which means 'the garden'

justice the idea that everyone has the right to be treated fairly

less economically developed countries (LEDCs) poor countries where most people struggle to survive

madrasah a school held at the mosque to teach children Arabic to help them read the Qur'an

mahr the dowry the groom pays to his future Muslim wife. It shows he respects her as a person in her own right and demonstrates that he can afford to keep a wife and children

marriage the condition of a man and woman legally united for the purpose of living together and, usually, having children

miracle something which seems to break a law of science and makes you think only God could have done it

monogamous being married or in a sexual relationship with one person only

moral evil actions done by humans which cause suffering

moral issues issues concerned with whether an action is right or wrong. Although the religions will have something to say about it, people who do not believe in any religion are also likely to have opinions about what is right and wrong. Issues such as abortion and stealing could be considered moral issues. These are also sometimes referred to as ethical issues

muezzin the man who calls Muslims to prayer

multi-ethnic society many different races and cultures living together in one society

multi-faith society many different religions living together in one society

mystical experience a spiritual feeling

natural evil things which cause suffering but have nothing to do with humans, e.g. earthquakes

nikah the Muslim marriage contract. It is essentially a business contract

non-voluntary euthanasia ending someone's life painlessly when they are unable to ask, but you have good reason for thinking they would want you to do so, e.g. switching off a life-support machine

nuclear family mother, father and children living as a unit

numinous the feeling of the presence of something greater than you, e.g. in a church or looking up at the stars

omnipotent the belief that God is all-powerful

omniscient the belief that God knows everything that has happened and everything that is going to happen

paranormal unexplained things which are thought to have spiritual causes, e.g. ghosts and mediums

pluralism different groups can coexist

polygamy being legally married to more than one person at a time

prayer an attempt to contact God, usually through words

prejudice believing some people are inferior or superior without even knowing them

pre-marital sex sex before marriage

promiscuity having sex with a number of partners without commitment

propaganda information given out by an organisation which is designed to persuade people to think along certain lines

purgatory a place where Catholics believe souls go after death to be purified

qurbani meat which has been given as a sacrifice in Islam

racial harmony different races/colours living together happily

racism the belief that some races are superior to others

Ramadan the ninth month when the Qur'an says all Muslims must fast

re-constituted family where two sets of children (step-brothers and sisters) become one family when their divorced parents marry each other

religious freedom the right to practise your religion or change your religion

religious issues issues which involve discussion about life and ultimate questions such as 'Why am I here?' or 'What happens when I die?' which religions may attempt to answer. Alternatively, more straightforward questions to do with the practises of one particular religious group such as 'Can a Muslim marry a divorcee?' or 'Should priests be celibate?' are also considered to be religious issues

religious pluralism accepting all religions as having an equal right to coexist

re-marriage marrying again after being divorced from a previous marriage

resurrection the belief that, after death, the body stays in the grave until the end of the world when it is raised

riba any form of lending or borrowing money at interest which is disapproved of (in Islam)

sadaqah a Muslim's voluntary donation to charity

sanctity of life the belief that life is holy and belongs to God

sawm fasting by going without food and drink during daylight hours (the fourth pillar)

sexism discriminating against people because of their gender (being male or female)

stewardship taking care of something that does not belong to you and using it wisely. Christians and Muslims believe that all wealth belongs to God and is given to us to use wisely

ummah the worldwide Muslim community, the nation of Islam

voluntary euthanasia the situation where someone dying in pain asks a doctor to end her/his life painlessly

walimah the Islamic family marriage reception that takes place after the signing of the nikah. This may not take place immediately after the signing of the nikah, but the couple do not usually live together until after the walimah, which is the public part of the wedding

worship-type programme a programme where the viewer can join in at home. They can sing or pray to God in the same way as they would in church. For the viewer, the programme is more than entertainment

wudu the ritual washing before prayer in Islam

zakah the third pillar of Islam. Muslims are required to give 2.5 per cent of their surplus wealth to charity

INDEX

Bold indicates a glossary entry. Italic indicates an exam focus question.

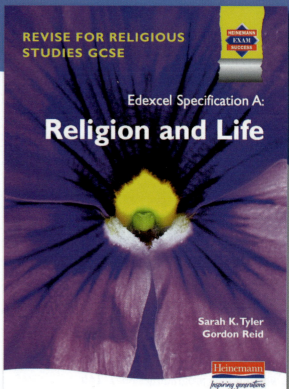
 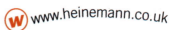